IMAGES
of America

THEATRES IN LOS ANGELES

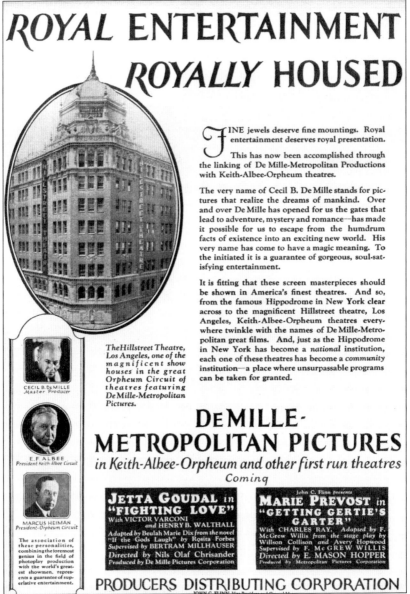

THEATRE ADVERTISEMENT. "Royal Entertainment Royally Housed" indeed, with "adventure, mystery and romance . . . gorgeous, soul-satisfying entertainment," courtesy of Cecil B. DeMille. The Hill-Street Theater was just a few years old in 1927 when this advertisement appeared, lauding DeMille's films as the type "that realize the dreams of mankind" in the "magnificent show houses" of Keith-Albee-Orpheum theatres, "a place where unsurpassable programs can be taken for granted."

ON THE COVER: The Bruin Theatre in Westwood Village has played host to gala film premieres since its opening in 1937. The overflowing crowd for the premiere of *The Adventures of Casanova* also filled the Fox Village across the street. A reviewer in 1948 called the film "historic balderdash." Maybe so, but it looked like quite the glamorous evening. (Courtesy of Bison Archives.)

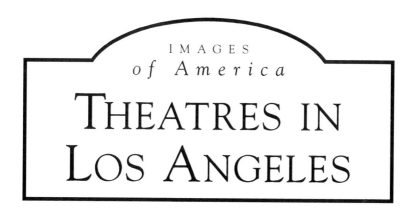

IMAGES
of America

THEATRES IN LOS ANGELES

Suzanne Tarbell Cooper,
Amy Ronnebeck Hall, and Marc Wanamaker

ARCADIA
PUBLISHING

Published by Arcadia Publishing
Charleston, South Carolina

Printed in the United States of America

Library of Congress Catalog Card Number: 2007931262

For all general information contact Arcadia Publishing at:
Telephone 843-853-2070
Fax 843-853-0044
E-mail sales@arcadiapublishing.com
For customer service and orders:
Toll-Free 1-888-313-2665

Visit us on the Internet at www.arcadiapublishing.com

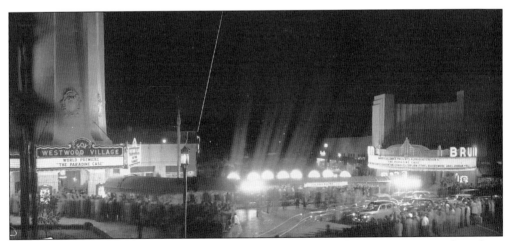

THE FOX WESTWOOD AND FOX BRUIN THEATRES. Were these dueling premieres or rivals working smoothly together? Southern California was once so densely peppered with playhouses that it could be hard to tell. Westwood's Bruin and Fox theatres still host star-studded openings, and over the years it has not been unusual for a film to premiere in both simultaneously.

CONTENTS

ACKNOWLEDGMENTS

Many thanks to all the wonderful people who have helped us, especially Rory Cunningham, J. Eric Lynxwiler, David Pacheco, Jerry Roberts, Stan Poe, Chris Launi, John Thomas, and the B'hend and Kaufmann Archives, whose theatre photograph collection has been donated to the Academy. Thank you to Arnold Emerson Ronnebeck whose strength never ceases to amaze. Extravagant thanks to Frank Cooper—we couldn't have done it without you—and Logan Cooper, a child of the computer age who would rather watch a movie than admire the theatre.

Unless otherwise specified, all photographs were supplied by Bison Archives. Many have never appeared in print before.

ABOUT THE AUTHORS

Suzanne Tarbell Cooper is a board member of the Art Deco Society of Los Angeles and a coauthor of *Los Angeles Art Deco, Long Beach Art Deco,* and the upcoming *Los Angeles West Adams.* Although a brief stint managing a movie theatre was her worst job ever, she retains a fondness for theatre architecture and the stories found within.

Amy Ronnebeck Hall received her bachelor of arts degree in American history/American studies from Stephens College in Columbia, Missouri, and is currently studying for a bachelor of arts degree in art history. She is a coauthor of *Los Angeles Art Deco* and is a board member of the Art Deco Society of Los Angeles.

Marc Wanamaker is a founding member of Hollywood Heritage, Beverly Hills Historical Society, Los Angeles City Historical Society, and the L.A. Conservancy, and is associated with Los Angeles County Museum of Art (LACMA) and the Academy of Motion Pictures Arts and Sciences. He also established Bison Archives, an important resource for historic photographs and resource library about film and Los Angeles history.

INTRODUCTION

Los Angeles and the movies grew up together. The temperate climate and sunny days of Southern California filled an important need for early cinema. Before the invention of modern movie lighting, films demanded daylight and lots of it. Scenery was also a major draw. There was no need for painted backdrops when mountains, oceans, plains and urban landscape were all within a day's drive, even in a Model T Ford. From the moment Cecil B. DeMille fled snowy New York in search of a location to film *The Squaw Man*, the region has been considered synonymous with the movies. Other places may have cinema, but only Hollywood has "The Movies" in capital letters, complete with stars, glamour, neon, and excitement.

"Nothing so forcefully illustrates the broadening of the horizon of the picture industry as the growth of the photoplay theatre," wrote influential critic Edwin Schallert in 1923. "From the tiny nickelodeon, with its score of casual guests, to the cinema temple, rising in monumental grandeur and attracting the multitudes of amusement-seekers, the trail of the celluloid has stretched ever onward. Greater and greater has been the space demanded for the shadows and the lambent light. Far and wide has their spell been flung. And with each rising tier of seats, each soaring archway, each climbing proscenium, the prominence of cinema achievement has been built higher and more secure."

Every main street in every town boasted a theatre by the early 1920s. It's only fitting that Los Angeles built more of them—and bigger and better. The home of the movies was incandescent. Over the years, the Los Angeles area has had so many theatres that no one book could chronicle them all. The magnificent movie palaces along Broadway still represent the highest concentration of vintage theatres in the world. Live performance is an important part of the city as well. Most early theatres showed movies as an adjunct to vaudeville. Gradually film dwarfed the singers and dancers and comedians on the stage, as more and more theatres became devoted to cinema alone. But what actor has not yearned to prove him or herself in front of a live audience? Los Angeles is also a legitimate theatre town. Many theatres have gone from film to stage and back several times, no matter which purpose the original builders had in mind.

Los Angeles, like the exact purpose of a theatre, does not lend itself to neat categories. Boundaries of the city, whose haphazard growth has surrounded and engulfed several smaller towns, are frequently vague. Spurts of growth and a total lack of reverence for the past have led to an untidy sprawl; older buildings nestle close to modern structures with no apparent rhyme or reason. Unlike other forms of architecture, many theatres have survived into this century. Some retain their original use, whether stage or screen, but many have been adapted into churches or swap meets. Some are pristine. Some are recognizable. Too many have been remodeled into obscurity or torn down for parking lots. Developers threaten to make this book outdated almost immediately as they demolish the old to build bigger and newer buildings, lining their pockets at the expense of the city's architectural heritage.

"A few years ago not a single film theatre could have stood beside those of the spoken drama in elaborateness." Schallert continued, "Now the picture theatre is second to none in size and adornments. From the standpoint of beauty it is often more enthralling because of the emphasis placed on the appeal to the eye." When did theatres become merely a place to sit in the dark and not somewhere to appreciate in the light as well? Some time in the modern era, entrepreneurs figured out that they could make more money by dividing patrons into multiplexes of plain, shoebox-sized rooms. Television, video, and computers grabbed the imagination of the populace, diminishing the role of the movie palace.

When the star of *Sunset Boulevard* Norma Desmond said, "It's the pictures that got small," her line could equally well have applied to the setting. Like a fast-food restaurant, a mall multiplex is intentionally anonymous, built to get as many people in and out with their overpriced popcorn as quickly as possible. The old theatres "had faces." Enchantment began on the terrazzo sidewalk and built through the entrancing lobbies to the breathtaking auditorium, the shore where audience met silver screen. New theatres may still show films, but it is to the old motion picture palaces that Hollywood turns for a grand, star-studded premiere.

"No wrecker's tool can rip away the mystique of a theatre," wrote Al Martinez in a eulogy for a theatre bulldozed in 1974. "There are too many ghosts."

Not all old theatres have specters waving their phantom arms in the box office, but all of them, intact or demolished, are haunted by their former grandeur. From the insubstantial glamour that danced on the screen to the audiences, waiting rapt in the dark for the show to begin, theatres have tales to tell. Savor their stories. Enjoy the exploration.

One

DOWNTOWN

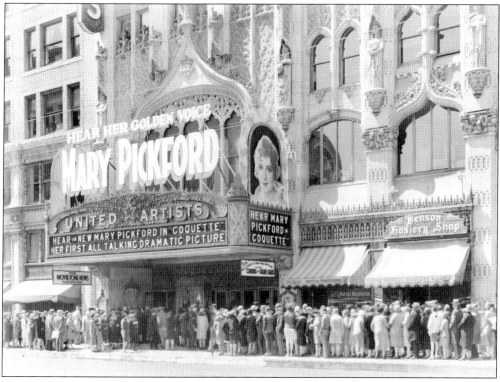

UNITED ARTISTS, 1929. How could the opening of United Artists flagship theatre at 933 South Broadway be anything but scintillating? Douglas Fairbanks rode the steam shovel, while Mary Pickford pulled the lever, lifting the first spade-full of earth at the star-studded ground breaking. Walker and Eisen with C. Howard Crane designed the height-limit building. Six hundred tons of polychrome and pulsichrome (a pseudo-granite) terracotta by Gladding-McBean faced the exterior. It was estimated that it would take one sculptor two years of constant labor to produce the tile, but scores of experts finished it in two months. The Florentine-style balcony was kept deliberately intimate in an auditorium that was huge, grand, and magnificent with gold. All 2,213 seats included additional spacing between rows to avoid the awkward shuffling of latecomers.

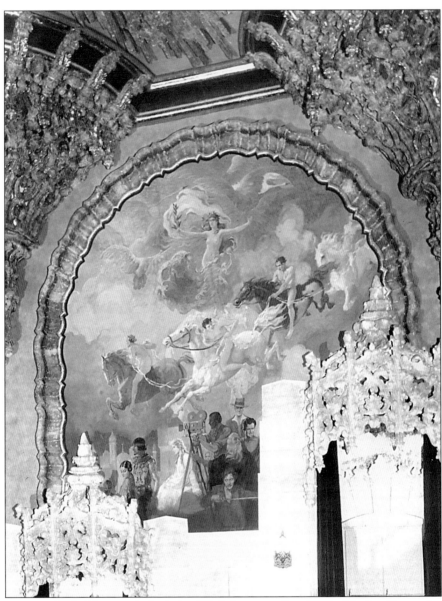

UA MURALS, 1929. The murals depicting "Enlightenment" and "The Motion Picture Industry Encircling the Globe" were lavishly praised and scolded by both stars and the press. Gloria Swanson objected to her first husband looking over her shoulder, so Wallace Beery was repainted into anonymity with a haircut, beard, and nose job. Sam Goldwyn was put out that Vilma Banky was omitted. A. B. Heinsberger, V. Ulianoff, and A. W. Parsons, with Jose Rivas, relegated Charlie Chaplin to a dark, inconspicuous corner, while Douglas Fairbanks was represented prominently twice, once as *Robin Hood*, and again as *The Thief of Bagdad*. Perhaps that is why one critic, while conceding that the murals were in good taste, wondered whether the motion-picture industry was in its infancy or its second childhood.

UA LOBBY, 1929. Excitement built as the building neared completion. The *Los Angeles Times* described it as "United Artist's Christmas gift to Los Angeles." Fashion spreads speculated on what 1927's starlets were expected to wear. The newspaper later described the premiere, featuring Mary Pickford in *My Best Girl*, as "Superbrilliant . . . with virtually all of the first magnitude stars of filmdom present."

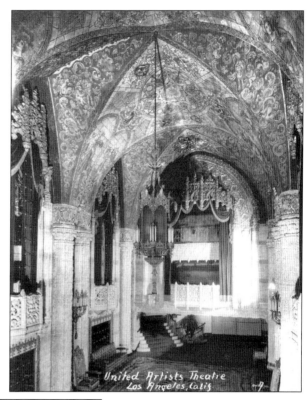

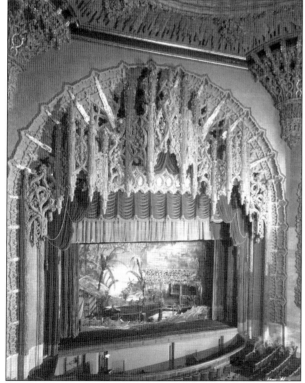

UNITED ARTISTS PROSCENIUM, 1929. This curtain's painted tropical shack seems rather out of place surrounded by such gilded splendor. Gossip columnist Myra Nye described it as "a background of glorious resplendence for the best that Hollywood can offer in the way of human beauty." It's now dedicated to a different glory: An illuminated, red "Jesus Saves" crowns Dr. Gene Scott's Los Angeles University Cathedral, caretaker of the building designed for movie royalty.

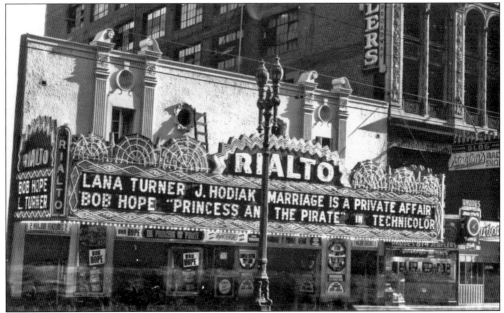

RIALTO, 1944. Not only did the 1917 opening benefit the Home Gardens Committee, which promoted gardening to stem wartime food shortages, but owner J. A. Quinn had the theatre's roof planted with vegetables, and encouraged other downtown buildings to do the same. Designed by Oliver P. Dennis, 812 South Broadway was remodeled in 1919 by William L. Woolett for Sid Grauman. The marquee was a 1930s addition.

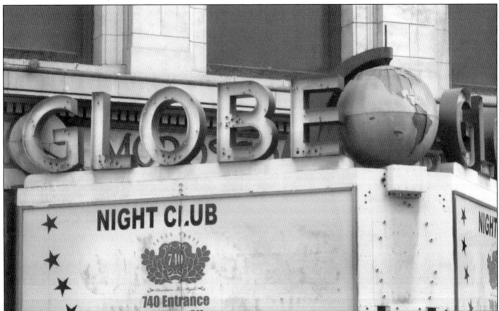

GLOBE THEATRE. There was some doubt that theatregoers in 1913 would venture as far uptown as 744 South Broadway, but the grandeur and comfort of the new Morosco Theatre won them over. Designed by Morgan and Walls with A. F. Rosenheim, the theatre was considered a stepping-stone to stardom. It has since been Los Angeles's first newsreel theatre, the Globe, and a swap meet, but the name "Morosco" is still visible. (Suzanne Cooper.)

TOWER THEATRE. S. Charles Lee's first theatre project, commissioned by independent exhibitor H. L. Gumbiner, opened in October 1972. With only a 50-foot-wide lot, they proved that one doesn't need a large piece of real estate to build a lavish theatre. Known as Newsreel for years, it was renamed Tower in 1965 by Gumbiners daughter and showed first-run features. Now closed, it is used for filming.

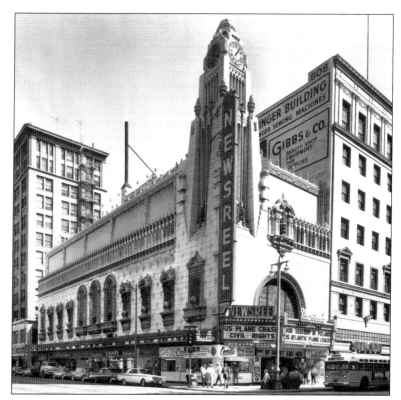

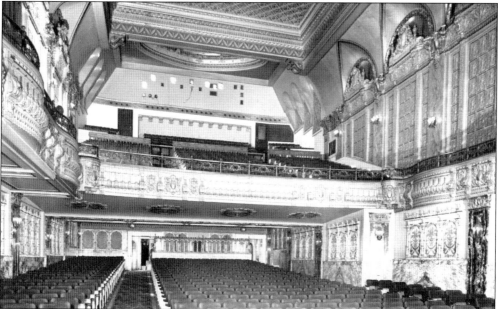

TOWER THEATRE AUDITORIUM, 1963. Located at 802 South Broadway, this theatre's elaborate French Renaissance style was an interpretation of the Paris Opera. The marble used throughout the theatre was imported from such varied locations as Italy, France, Alaska, and Vermont. Comfort was also in the air; their advertisements read, "Manufactured Weather makes every day a good day at the Tower Theatre."

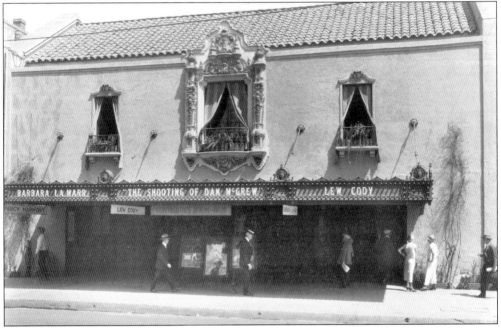

MISSION THEATRE, 1924. Built on the site of the Victory Theatre in 1920 and demolished six years later to build the Orpheum, the Mission Theatre is a bit of a mystery. Plans called for a public tearoom and a pool with water cascading over glass. The opening picture was Douglas Fairbanks's *The Mark of Zorro*. Was it just "bigger is better" or a time-lost story that caused the theatre's demise?

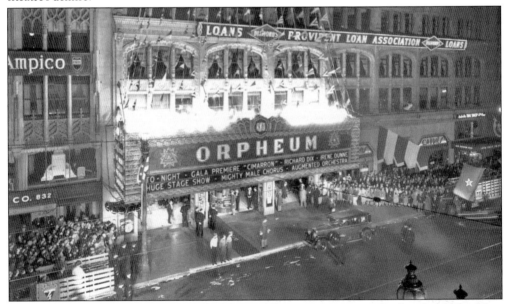

ORPHEUM THEATRE, 1931. In 1925, the Mission Theatre gave way to the fourth and final Los Angeles Orpheum at 842 South Broadway. Originally constructed as a vaudeville theatre, it had to change with the times and began showing films in the very early 1930s. *Cimarron* had its gala premiere there on February 8, 1931. This is also the home of the last remaining Mighty Wurlitzer on Broadway.

ORPHEUM THEATRE, 1952. After its gala opening on February 15, 1926, the Orpheum continued to exhibit vaudeville, cinema, and live-music acts. Most shows claimed to be the best thing since sliced bread, although none more so than the premiere of Cecil B. DeMille's *Greatest Show on Earth*. The marquee shown here dates from the mid-1930s. The theatre was renovated in 2001.

ORPHEUM INTERIOR. From 1894–1896, G. Albert Lansburgh worked as a draftsman for Bernard Maybeck and later graduated with honors from L'Ecole des Beaux Arts in Paris. His time in France clearly influenced his French baroque design for the Orpheum. He was on the architectural commission for the 1915 Pacific Exposition in San Diego. After a lengthy career designing landmarks throughout California, Lansburgh died in 1969.

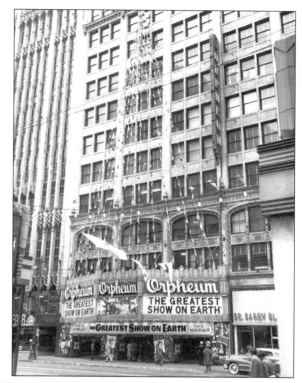

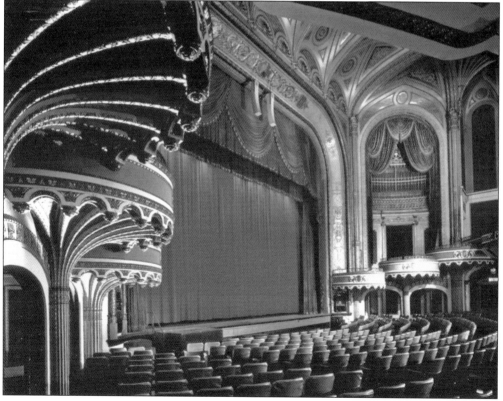

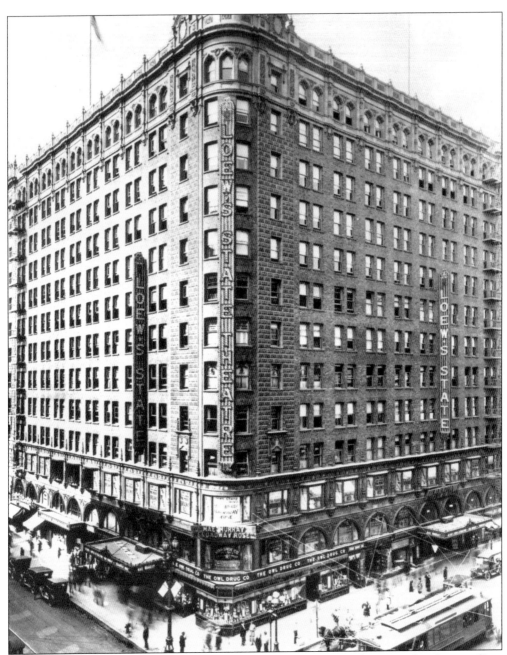

LOEW'S STATE, 1922. The intersection of Seventh Street and Broadway was already one of Los Angeles's busiest, so when an estimated 10,000 people showed up for the November 1921 opening of the Loew's State, no one was shocked. Downtown was gridlocked, with spectators hanging out hotel windows trying to glimpse Hollywood notables. The opening night was chockablock with entertainment media, including an orchestra concert, film premiere of *The Trip to Paradise*, and several vaudeville acts. The structure is steel and concrete with a red brick veneer. In keeping with the Spanish Revival style of the architecture, the usherettes wore traditional Spanish garb filtered through 1920s sensibilities. Shown here in 1922, this is architects Charles P. Weeks and William Day's only theatre in the Los Angeles area. Most of their work is in Northern California.

LOEW'S STATE, 1946. The State was part of film exhibitor Marcus Loew's then-growing empire, which included both the United States and Canada. Loew purchased Metro Pictures in 1920 and in 1924 merged it with Samuel Goldwyn and Louis B. Mayer's companies to form MGM. Loew's State has been a Spanish-language cinema and home to a religious organization.

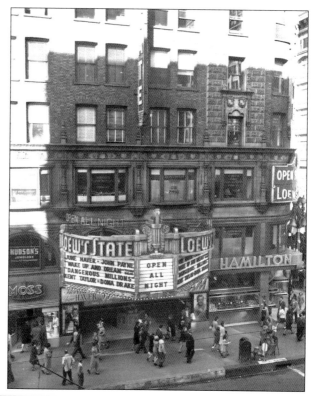

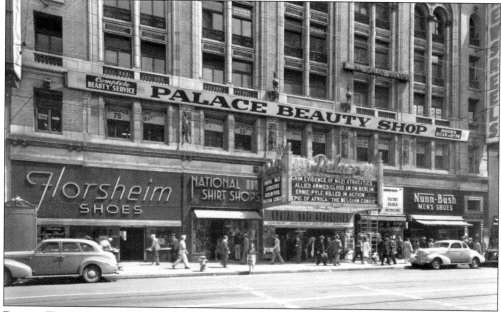

PALACE THEATRE, 1945. Opened as the Orpheum in 1911, and designed by G. Albert Lansburgh, the Palace evolved with technology, presenting vaudeville shows, silent films, and talkies. The exterior of 630 South Broadway showcases relief sculptures of the Muses of Vaudeville by Domingo and Jose Mora. The interior features French influences and pastel colors, an escape from the grim realities of World War II.

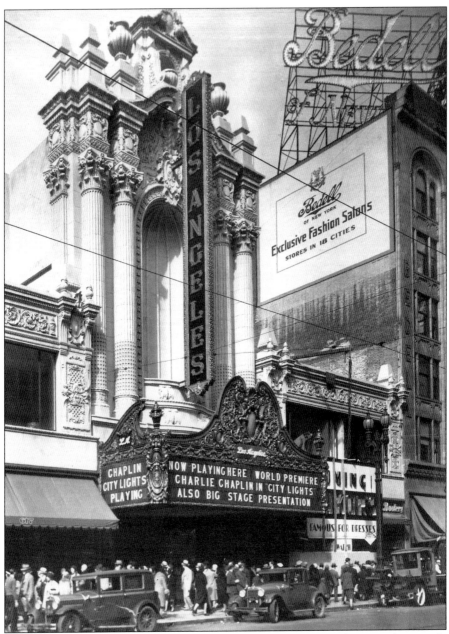

LOS ANGELES THEATRE, 1931. Although talkies had been the rage for several years, the Los Angeles opened in January 1931 with a silent film. Because Charlie Chaplin's *City Lights* was unfavorably received during previews, and because he had produced the film independently, Chaplin had difficulty persuading a theatre to show it. Independent exhibitor H. L. Gumbiner, owner of the Los Angeles Theatre, came to Chaplin's rescue. The lavishness of the new theatre at 615 South Broadway was matched only by the glamour of premiere attendees, such as Albert Einstein and Gloria Swanson. Crowds swelled to an estimated 25,000 people and were difficult for the police to control. Poor impecunious souls watched from the breadline across the street as premiere attendees paid $10 to see a movie. Bread was 8¢ a loaf, and the price of admission would have paid for a lot of it . . . or let them eat cake.

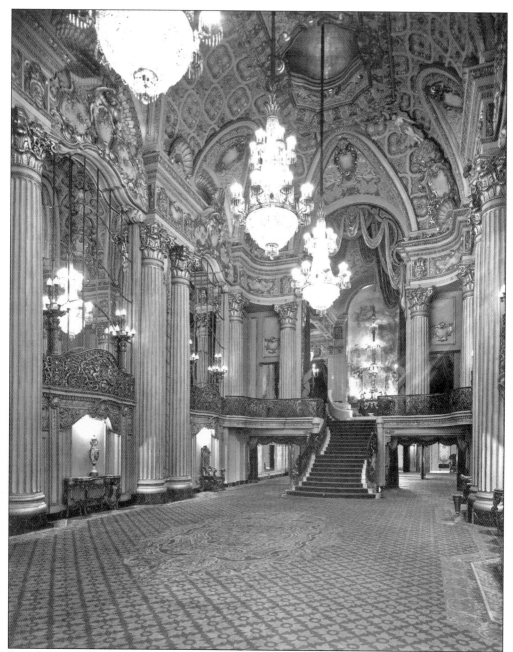

LOS ANGELES INTERIOR, 1931. S. Charles Lee was the architect behind this building's French renaissance-inspired design, modeled after the Hall of Mirrors at Versailles. The lobby was six stories tall with a barrel-vaulted ceiling, flowing draperies, and crystal chandeliers. The graceful grand staircase led to the mezzanine level, where one would be greeted by a crystal fountain. All of this grandeur also served a very practical purpose: distraction. Theatergoers could forget, at least for a short while, the bleak reality of the Depression. Unfortunately that wouldn't be the case for owner H. L. Gumbiner, who was never able to break the monopoly the studios had in exhibiting first-run films. He was forced to declare bankruptcy, and the theatre closed only 10 months later. It is now only open for filming and special events.

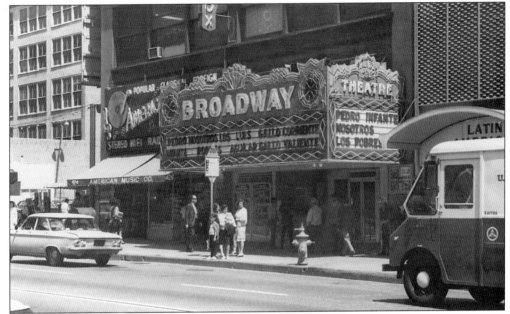

BROADWAY THEATRE, 1967. Sherrill C. Corwin became manager of his father's theatre at 428 South Broadway in 1923. He remembered it as "a haberdashery store, a nickelodeon kind of thing." As the composition of downtown changed, it became the first theatre in the Metropolitan chain to show Spanish-language films. The next-door neighbor, American Music, opened in 1940 with a customer giveaway: a recording of each visitor's own voice, talking, singing, or whistling.

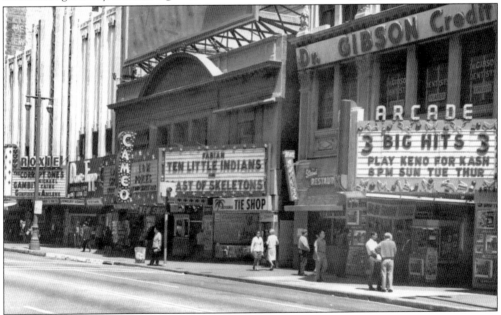

ARCADE THEATRE, 1967. Carved in stone above the doors is a clue to the Arcade's 1910 origins: "Pantages." The Morgan and Walls building built for the legendary showman, at 534 South Broadway, now fronts retail space. In the early 1930s, theatre bombings spread across the country. Although the theatre denied labor friction, the unknown assailant who hurled a stench bomb at a burlesque dancer was probably not a crazed moralist but a unionist making a violent point.

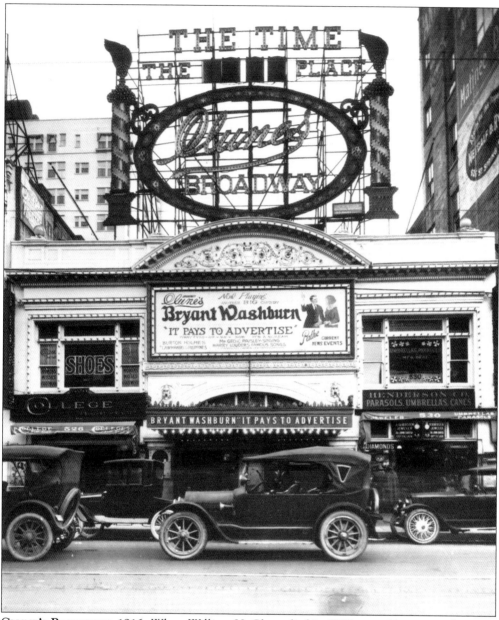

CLUNE'S BROADWAY, 1916. When William H. Clune died in 1927, one of his many obituaries described him as a man who developed the movie house from "the old nickelodeon theatre with its bare walls, hard wooden seats and tinkling piano to the motion-picture palace with its ... luxurious fittings." Clune's Broadway Theatre, designed in 1910 by Alfred Rosenheim, was a forerunner of the opulent theatres awaiting audiences in the next decades. After Clune's retirement in 1923, a group of 50 workmen under the direction of William Cutts transformed the venerable building at 528 South Broadway into a modern, air-cooled motion-picture house. The manager promised, "The best and most luxuriously appointed 'small' theatre on Broadway." Mural artists added wall paintings and cabinetmakers carved intricate grills as the theatre gained a larger lobby and a few more seats. A Hollywood man won $25 and an annual pass to the theatre with his prize-winning name: the Cameo Theatre.

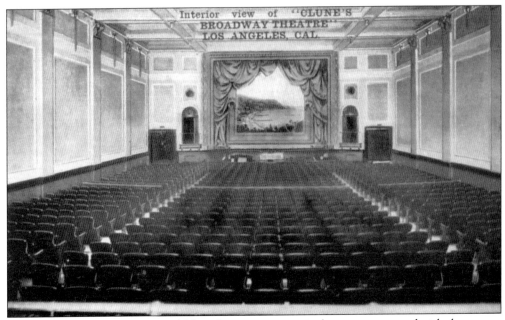

CLUNE'S BROADWAY INTERIOR. Although it seems surprisingly sparse compared with the rococo palaces that followed it, Clune's Broadway was state-of-the-art luxury in 1910, with paneled ceilings and a large central skylight. The proscenium was designed to allow the exhibition of pictures in a larger format than was customary at the time. (Newman Post Card Company, courtesy of Rory Cunningham.)

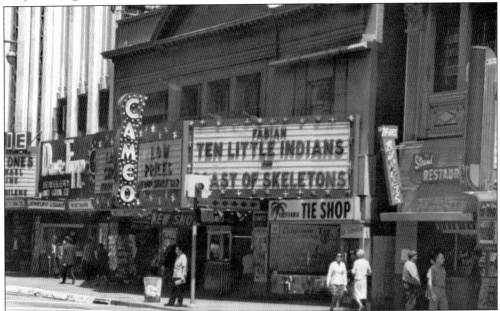

CAMEO THEATRE, 1967. The theatres along Broadway lost favor as the city's population became increasingly suburban. By 1978, the Cameo had fallen to pornographic films. Looking for remnants of the past in the triple-X-rated theatre, Jack Smith wrote, "Everything had been painted a lifeless brown. I strained my eyes up to the ceiling . . . There had been angels once, pink angels in a pale blue sky . . . I remembered them myself from the '30s."

ROXIE THEATRE. Designed by architect John M. Cooper in 1931, this theatre at 518 South Broadway was the last one built in the downtown theatre district. Because of its relatively late date, its Art Deco design makes it unique in relation to the other theatres in the area. It is now used for a swap meet and few original details remain. (Frank E. Cooper Jr.)

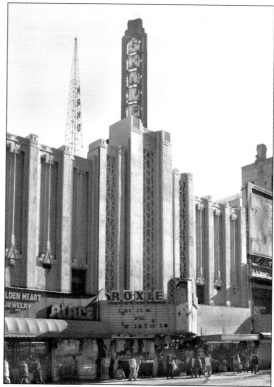

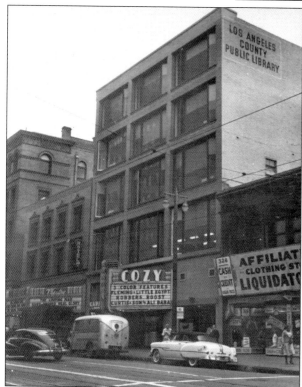

COZY THEATRE, 1955. It's easy to see how the Cozy Theatre got its name. The 350-seat theatre, once at 320 South Broadway, was designed by Albert C. Martin in 1927. By 1960, kids dared one another to scream happily through quadruple bills of monster movies, smarter than the 1945 youth who accepted a dare to snatch box office receipts. His prize was a police bullet and a trip to jail.

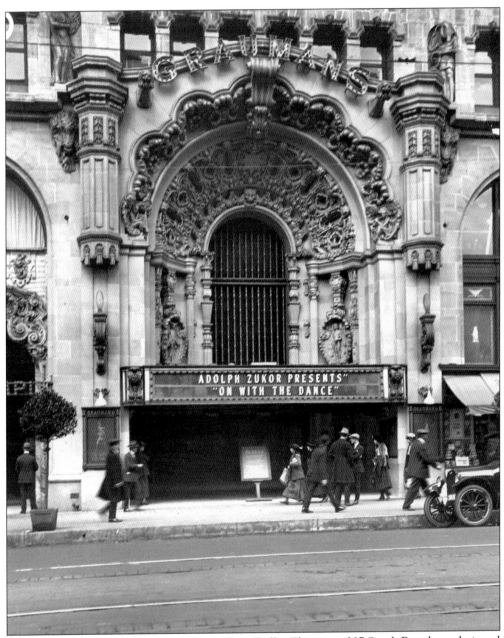

MILLION DOLLAR THEATRE, 1920. The Million Dollar Theatre at 307 South Broadway, designed by William J. Woolett, is the site of a momentous first: Master Showman Sid Grauman's first theatre in Los Angeles. The premiere film was *The Silent Man*, starring William S. Hart. The gala opening on February 1, 1918, was a pure Grauman event, with thousands in attendance, including Charlie Chaplin, Douglas Fairbanks, and Fatty Arbuckle. Since Grauman was well known for elaborate prologues, he made sure the theatre design included enhancements needed for stage productions. The audience amenities included seats 20 inches wide and staggered for clear views, luxurious lounges, furnishings, and decorations. Many original elements, such as the Grauman's sign, have been removed. The original marquee was replaced. Perhaps its current refurbishing will restore them.

MILLION DOLLAR THEATRE, 1924. Albert C. Martin Sr. designed the Million Dollar's Edison Building in the Churrigueresque style. Sculptures in the third-level niches are film-industry-themed dancers and actors. On the Third Street side, Joseph Mora executed fanciful sculptures of the American West, including bison heads, Texas longhorn skulls, and six-shooter pistols. The floors above held offices, including those of William Mulholland and the Metropolitan Water District.

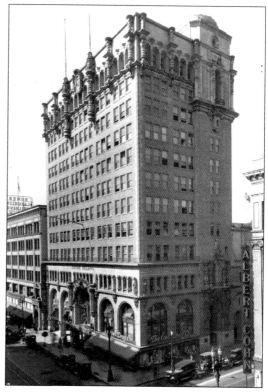

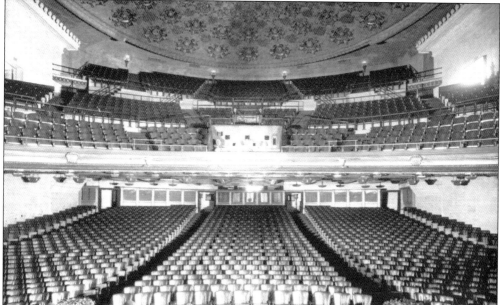

MILLION DOLLAR THEATRE AUDITORIUM, 1918. Sid Grauman wanted to know how many people were in the theatre at all times, so he had the "Hansen seating device" installed. Like a telephone switchboard, each seat had a sensor connected to a panel in Grauman's office and a cabinet visible only to the ushers. Empty seats triggered a light that allowed ushers to seat patrons and Grauman to estimate attendance.

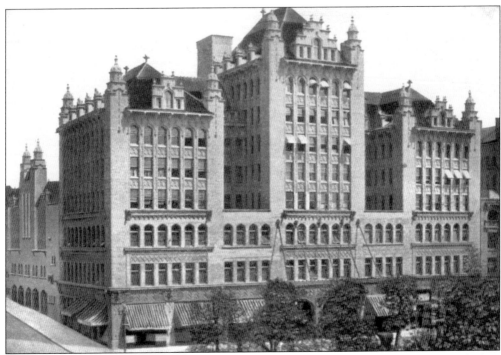

PHILHARMONIC AUDITORIUM. The "Auditorium Theatre Beautiful" opened in 1906, a grand gift to the growing city designed by Charles Whittlesey that overlooked a lush, green Pershing Square. Later Clune added his name to the roofline at Fifth and Olive Streets. In 1920, it became Philharmonic Hall, official home of the Los Angeles Philharmonic. Now the site is called "Parking Lot" and adjoins the city's ugliest all-concrete park. (Newman Postcard, courtesy of Rory Cunningham.)

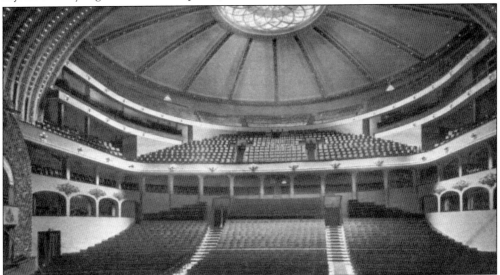

PHILHARMONIC AUDITORIUM INTERIOR. Although the 1938 remodel is generally attributed to Stiles O. Clements, an intriguing link suggests that Claud Beelman may have had a hand in it. A March 1938 *Los Angeles Times* article credits him with "the modern architectural design and details of the interior," and his name is on several building permits for the year this interior, shown in its earlier incarnation, was updated. (M. Rieder, courtesy of Rory Cunningham.)

PHILHARMONIC AUDITORIUM. Remodeling was bittersweet for impresario L. E. Behymer when he lost the attic office where he entertained artists from Sousa to Nijinsky. "The old building is going to have her face lifted," he said wistfully. "Workmen are going to raise the roof. I raised the roof when I found I would have to move, but I've been subdued by arguments about making way for progress." (Courtesy of Rory Cunningham.)

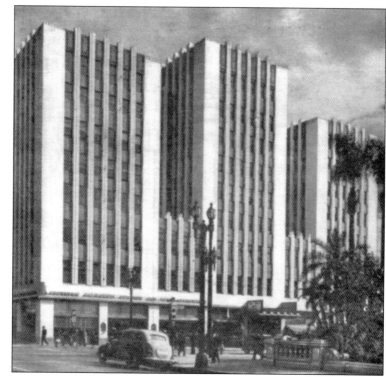

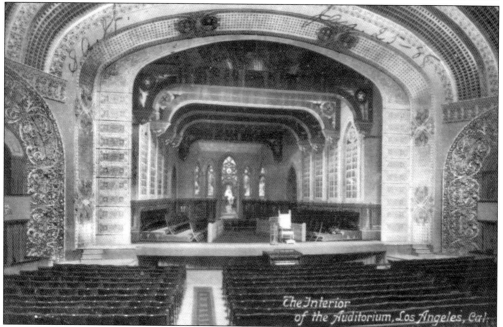

PHILHARMONIC AUDITORIUM INTERIOR. Lynden Ellsworth Behymer, affectionately known as "Bee," managed the Philharmonic, as well most major theatres in Los Angeles, throughout his 60-year career. After his death in 1947, his widow continued his work. The couple began their careers in 1888, two decades before the curtain first rose in the building most simply called "The Auditorium." (M. Rieder, courtesy of Rory Cunningham.)

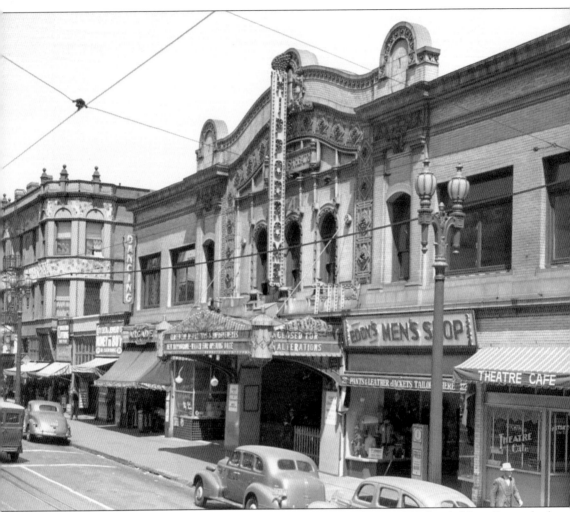

HIPPODROME THEATRE, 1940. When the Hippodrome Theatre, 320 South Main Street, had its first birthday in 1914, the manager threatened to write a book about what he had learned, including the need to understand human beings and actors. His opinion? "The former is easy compared to the latter." Before the theatre opened in 1911 as the Adolphus, its first manager, with equal cynicism, declared his preference for moneymaking melodrama, saying he would "much prefer *Bertha, The Beautiful Sewing Machine Girl* to *Hedda Gabler*." In 1952, the theatre lovingly nicknamed "The Hip," was demolished and replaced by a parking lot. The *Los Angeles Times* described the 3,500-pound ball of steel and cast iron felling one of the city's largest theatres, which "crumbled to earth . . . in a cloud of powdery concrete." Still, it existed longer than a competing theatre across the street that closed after six weeks because a persistent ghost apparently gnashed teeth, terrifying performers (who may have been more ghost-tolerant if they had been paid for their work).

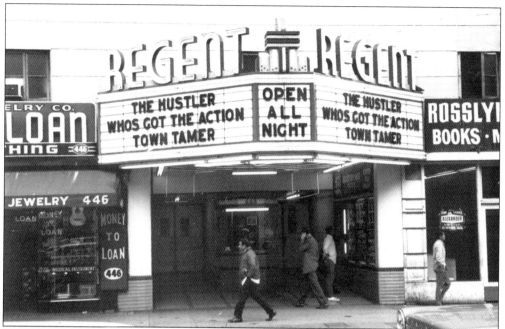

REGENT THEATRE, 1967. In 1918, in a vigorous campaign to rid Los Angeles of indecent movies, the city prosecutor's office seized a film at the Banner Theatre, 446–448 South Main Street. Four years later, the owner's wife began divorce proceedings, claiming her husband wrote the following poetry for a cashier: " 'Twas a perfect day, we chatted and cooed." Perhaps she got the theatre in the settlement, as by 1924 it had become the Regent.

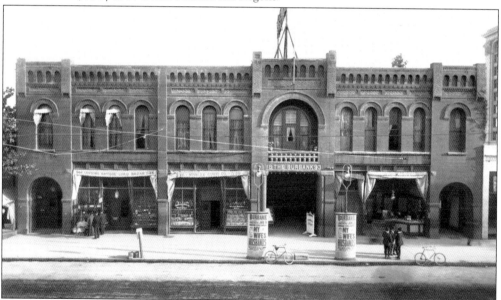

BURBANK THEATRE, 1893. Once the pride of the dentist who founded Burbank, the memory of Robert Brown Young's 1893 theatre now haunts a parking lot at 548 South Main Street. Another ghost could be the man who invaded the nighttime theatre with twisted love for a showgirl. He shot himself in an eerie flood of light in the place she would dance, next to his chalked message, which read, "Good-by, Angel Face!"

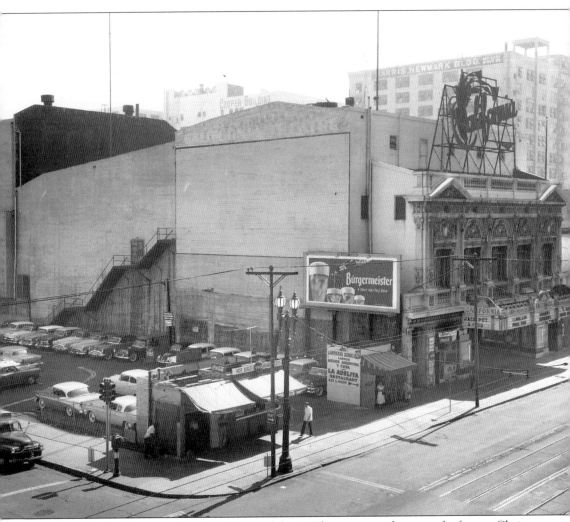

CALIFORNIA THEATRE, 1956. Miller's California Theatre opened to great fanfare on Christmas Eve 1918. The *Los Angeles Times* gushed about the 24 ushers in "blue-gray garments chosen from the uniforms of the Allied armies" who led a veritable who's who of silent film—Charlie Chaplin, Mary Pickford, Cecil B. DeMille, Douglas Fairbanks, and others—from the magic carpet inlaid in the floor of the foyer to their seats in the ornate new theatre at 810 South Main Street. Architect A. B. Rosenthal had designed the theatre to be strong as well as beautiful. The balcony was tested with 18,000 bags of cement, demonstrating that it would be capable of safely holding 1.8 million pounds or a maximum of 12,000 people, although its capacity was only 1,600. It couldn't withstand the forces of change, however, and the theatre, balcony and all, was eventually demolished.

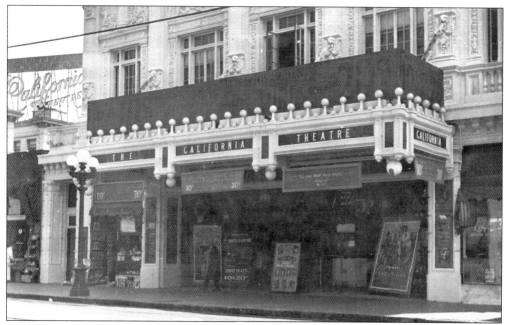

CALIFORNIA THEATRE, 1928. Not a bad day out: For 10 to 20¢, the California Theatre offered vaudeville plus a moving picture. After the show, a lady could go next door to California Artistic Haircutting to have her tresses styled like Gloria Swanson's while her husband shopped for cigars at the tobacco shop on the other side of the theatre.

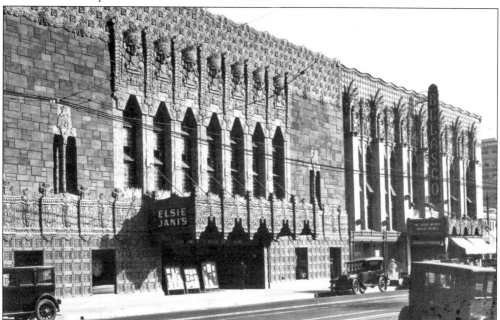

MAYAN THEATRE, 1927. Built by the Belasco Theatre chain, this building was designed by the architectural firm of Morgan, Walls and Clements. The Mayan-themed interior and exterior decoration was conceived and executed by Mexican artist Francisco Cornejo. The facade is cast concrete and was originally an unembellished gray. In August 1927, Elsie Janis starred in the Mayan's premiere production, *Oh Kay*, a musical comedy about Prohibition.

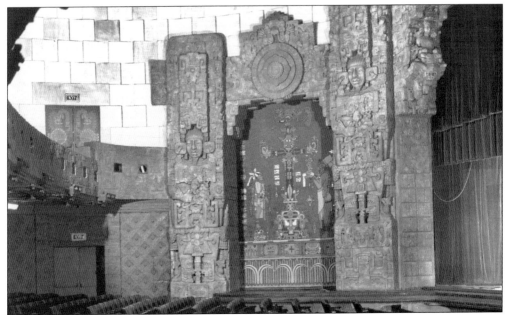

MAYAN THEATRE INTERIOR, 1935. Francisco Cornejo was fascinated by pre-Columbian art and both promoted and worked in that style throughout his career. Born in Mexico City, Cornejo lived in Los Angeles from 1911 to 1930. He believed that since Mayan- and Aztec-style art and architecture were native to continental soil, they were far more appropriate influences than Eurocentric style art, which was and still is the tradition.

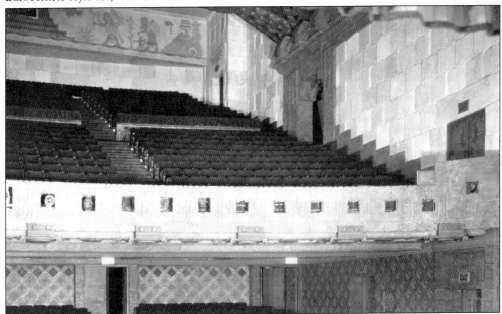

MAYAN THEATRE BALCONY. The flamboyant structure at 1038 South Hill Street has led several lives. Since the Belasco chain also operated the theatre next door, its initial booking policy for the Mayan focused strictly on musical comedy. That soon gave way to films, first in English, then Spanish, and eventually XXX. The seats were removed and a false floor added to cover the rake when the Mayan became a nightclub.

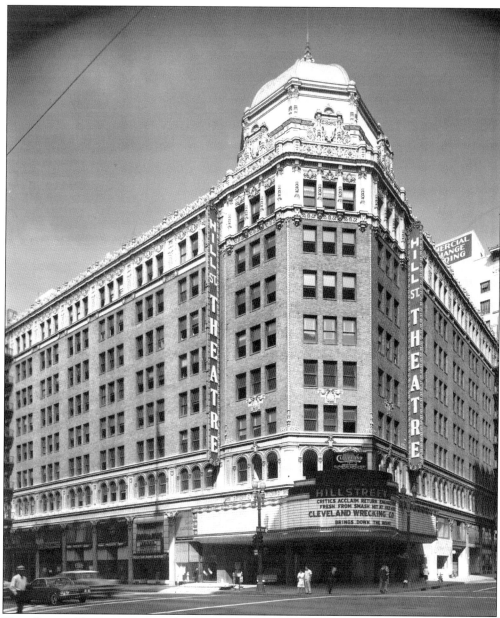

HILL-STREET THEATRE, 1965. The Hill-Street Theatre had a most unusual opening in 1922: the doors opened, the crowd entered, and the show began. Given the lack of ceremony, the first film, *Why Announce Your Marriage?* could easily have been re-titled *Why Announce Your Theater?* G. Albert Lansburgh designed the eight-story building at the southwest corner of Eighth and Hill Streets for the Junior Orpheum Circuit. Popular from the start, the theatre featured the usual array of movies and vaudeville performances with singers, dancers, comedians, and jugglers. In 1923, at the 13th anniversary celebration of the Boy Scouts of America, it premiered an official new handshake that would leave the right hand free for salutes and carrying the flag. In 1929, the theatre was redecorated and renamed the RKO Hillstreet. Sadly, in 1965, the marquee announced its final act: "Critics Acclaim Return Engagement, Fresh From Smash Hit at Biltmore, Cleveland Wrecking Company Brings Down the House."

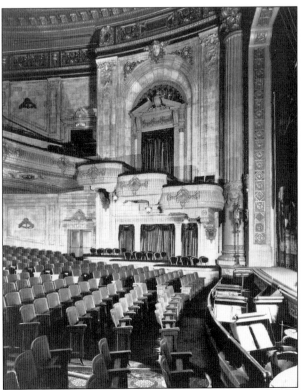

PANTAGES DOWNTOWN INTERIOR, 1920. Born in Greece, Alexander Pantages led a colorful life, beginning his entertainment career producing shows for the miners during the Klondike gold rush in the late 19th century. In a review of opening night, the *Los Angeles Times* wrote, "The adornments of the theatre were planned with a view towards permanency of their appeal." Appealing, yes. Permanence, no. Most of the original decorative features have been removed.

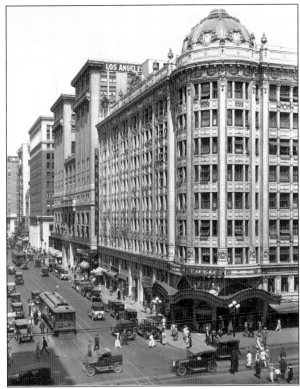

PANTAGES DOWNTOWN, 1920. Opened in August 1920, this was the second vaudeville theatre in Los Angeles to benefit from Pantages's golden touch. Designed by B. Marcus Priteca, the building's blend of classic styles included Greek revival and Italian renaissance, a style the impresario pronounced "Pantages Greek." Located at 401 West Seventh Street at Hill Street, the corner theatre is gracefully rounded and topped with a baroque dome.

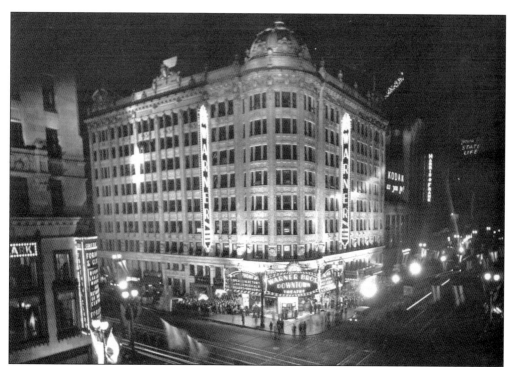

WARNER BROTHERS DOWNTOWN. While gold may have given Pantages his start, in September 1929, it would be a reminder of his failure. After Pantages sold his theatre chain in 1929, this theatre reopened as the Warner Brothers Downtown. Its premiere film was the musical *Golddiggers of Broadway*. There is still gold there, but one has to pay for it, as it is now a jewelry mart.

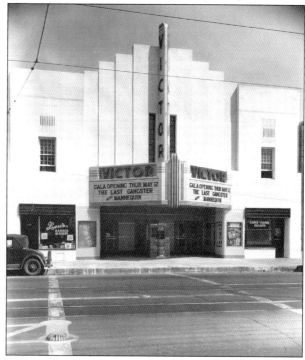

VICTOR THEATRE, 1938. Not even advertisements point to the passing of the Victor Theatre at 1718 South Main Street, but building permits show that it was built for moving pictures in 1912 and that West Coast Theatres did electrical work in 1925. It wasn't a drive-in theatre in its heyday but it is now one to drive over, as the site is buried under tons of concrete forming the Santa Monica Freeway.

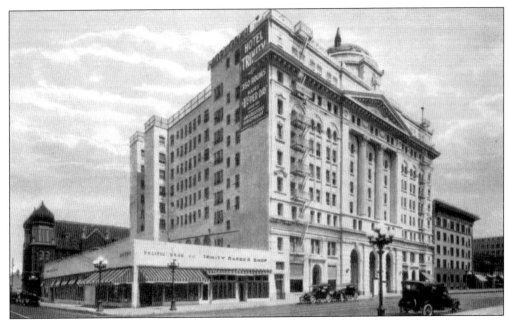

TRINITY AUDITORIUM. Most theatres don't feature a baptism on opening day, but Thornton Fitzhugh, Frank G. Krucker, and H. C. Deckbar planned Trinity as a sanctuary for the Methodist Episcopal church, as well as a showcase for musicians. Reverend Selecman preached, "Human hearts have not changed, but they are keeping time to the drumbeat of the twentieth century . . . the world wants an electric-lighted, self-starting, six-cylinder church." (E. C. Kropp, courtesy of Rory Cunningham.)

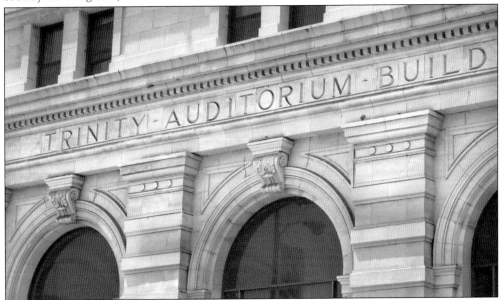

TRINITY AUDITORIUM. The nine-story building at Grand Avenue and Ninth Street once hosted religious services, union meetings, the philharmonic, opera, jazz, and rock. Although renamed the Embassy for many years, "Trinity" has been the name carved above the doors since 1914. The interior, topped by a stained-glass dome, included a hotel with, in Selecman's words, everything necessary to take a man "from the shower bath to the pearly gates." (Suzanne Cooper.)

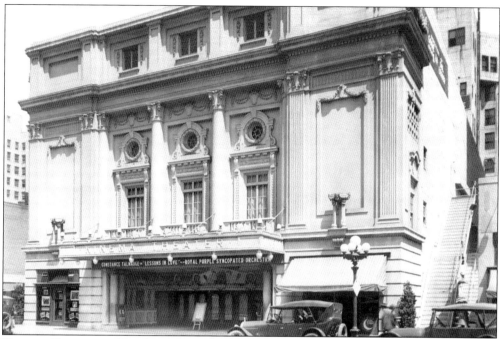

KINEMA THEATRE, 1921. As with much of history, the Kinema Theatre, grandly designed by Dodd and Richards in 1917 at 642 South Grand Avenue, exists only in memory. Charlie Chaplin premiered *A Woman of Paris* at its gala reopening as the Criterion in 1923, but President Hoover stayed in Washington when photographs of his inauguration, rushed from Washington as soon as they were dry, first appeared on the big screen.

GRANADA THEATRE, 1942. Now a church at 1042–1044 Temple Street, the Granada was once the Owl Theatre. In 1914, they advertised, "Complete change of pictures and special attractions every day—Always 5 Cents." The single-story brick building was damaged by fire in 1930, not an unusual occurrence with highly flammable film stock. A year earlier, they sued the city for damages, arguing that widening Temple Street would take 155 seats.

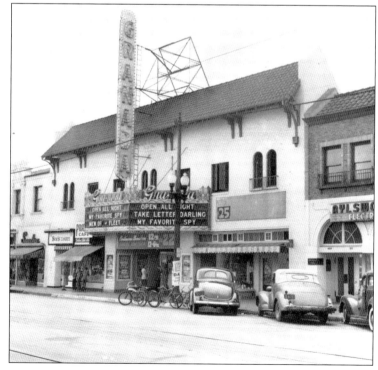

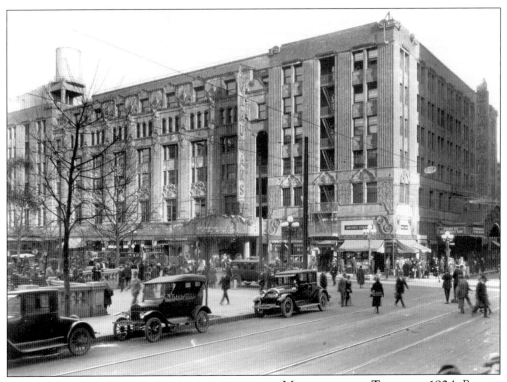

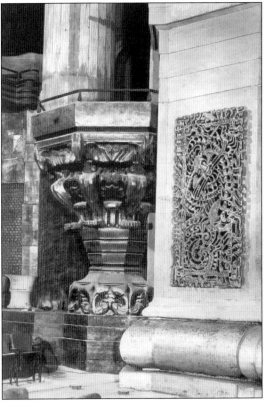

METROPOLITAN THEATRE, 1924. Reams of print hailed the opening of Grauman's Metropolitan in 1923. The elaborate theatre, by William Lee Woollett, was described in loving detail. The press was tepid about the opening attractions, however, commenting with little favor on the paucity of stars on the stage. The opening feature, *My American Wife,* was deemed not grand enough, although Gloria Swanson was lauded for both her popularity and her wardrobe.

METROPOLITAN THEATRE AUDITORIUM. The theatre itself was another story. Police and militia prevented rioting as crowds pressed in every direction from Sixth and Hill Streets, hoping for a brush with celebrity or a glimpse of the sumptuous interior, its seats dwarfed by massive decorations. Sid Grauman, it is said, wept at the opening but soon lost interest and transferred his passion to his new theatre in Hollywood. (Courtesy of J. Eric Lynxwiler.)

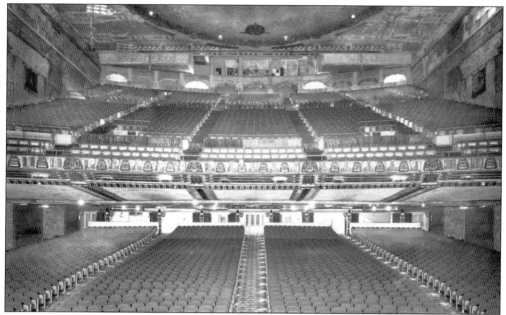

METROPOLITAN THEATRE AUDITORIUM. Opening night included a bewildering array of music in a space so vast one actor remarked, "I feel about an inch high." The national anthem was sung by Uncle Sam, accompanied by a marine, sailor, soldier, and a Red Cross nurse. This performance was followed by Wagner's *Grand March* from *Tannhaueser*, jazz by Waring's Pennsylvanians, and *Ave Maria* performed by forty violins and eight harps, punctuated by shouts from the crowd outside.

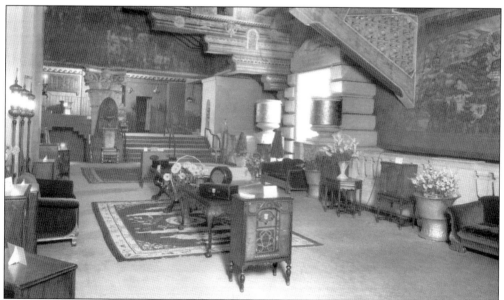

METROPOLITAN THEATRE LOBBY. The lobby looks bewitchingly cozy for such a grand theatre. A mural illustrates the story of the Princess of the Flowery Kingdom, imprisoned by a wicked magician in a bronze bell. Her affianced husband thwarted the spell with the help of a friendly spirit and a magic talisman. Bronze flowed to the ground around her feet, the dainty princess was freed and, presumably, she lived happily ever after.

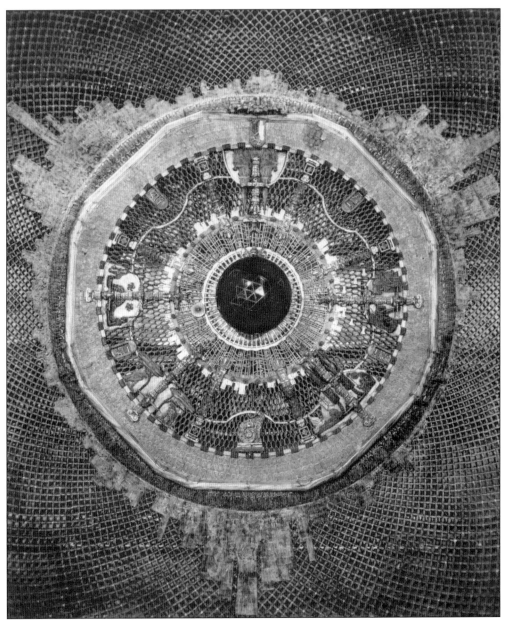

METROPOLITAN THEATRE CEILING DETAIL. Usherettes wore Grecian-inspired costumes from the same Japanese silk chiffon velvet that made up the curtains and batiks. The girls were real, but stone and marble in the lobby, and the plush cloth at the base of the pillars was concrete with a faux finish. Throughout much of the theatre, the concrete was left unpolished, revealing the grain of the boards used for molds. The crude edges that oozed from between the boards were sometimes emphasized with gold leaf. A lacy, 90-foot disc covering the greater part of the theatre ceiling was dubbed "the doily" by the men who built it. Thousands of incandescent bulbs of various colors glimmered through its deceptively delicate golden strips of lattice. The Metropolitan Theatre became the Paramount in 1929. In 1962, its sturdy construction—strong enough to support a building several times its size—created headaches for the wrecking crew charged with tearing it down to put up an office building. (Courtesy of J. Eric Lynxwiler.)

Two

MID-CITY

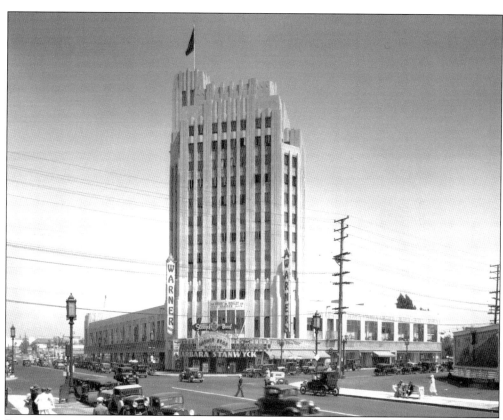

THE WILTERN THEATRE, 1932. Formerly the Warner Brothers Western and clad in vibrant Gladding-McBean blue-green tile, the Pellesier Building and theatre were designed to attract the attention of pedestrians, automobile drivers, and bus passengers alike. Located at the busy corner of Wilshire Boulevard at Western Avenue, sited diagonally, and only 12 stories tall, its clever 1930–1931 design by Morgan, Walls and Clements fools the eye into believing it is far taller.

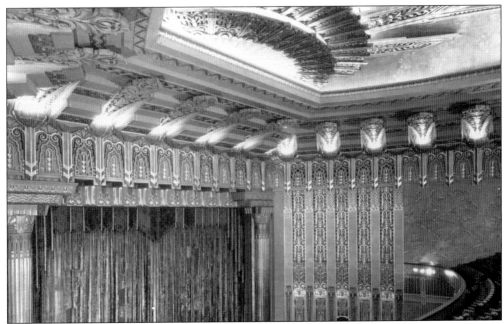

WILTERN THEATRE AUDITORIUM, 1931. The theatre's lush decoration, which included scrolls and chevrons, was by G. Albert Lansburgh. By the late 1970s, neglect allowed portions of the dramatic plaster sunburst to fall to the floor. The Los Angeles Conservancy was instrumental in saving the Art Deco treasure from the wrecking ball in the early 1980s. The sunburst was simplified during restoration.

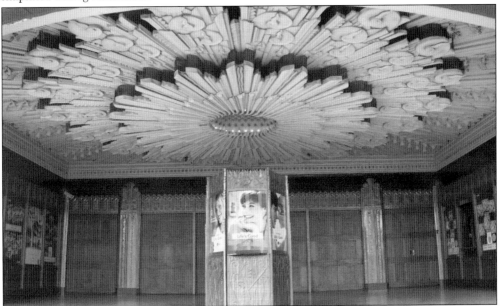

WILTERN THEATRE EXTERIOR LOBBY. Echoing the sun rays above is a floor made from terrazzo, a material made from marble and stone chips embedded into mortar. An ancient technique, the making of terrazzo was popularized in the United States in the 1920s. To handle larger crowds after the restoration, a new box office was created from an adjacent commercial space, but the original box office is far more elegant. (Frank E. Cooper Jr.)

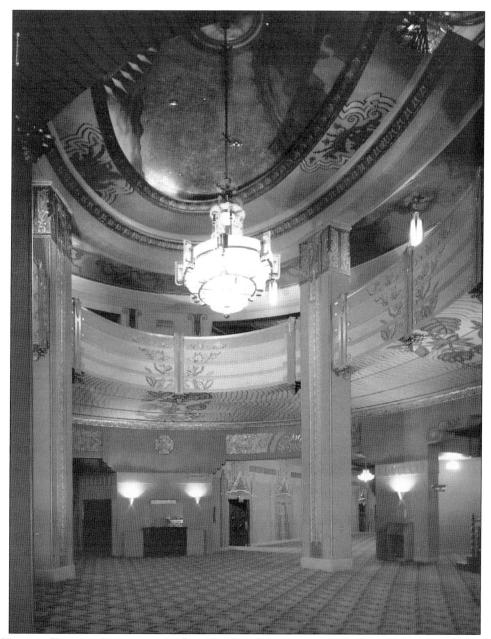

WILTERN THEATRE ROTUNDA. Anthony B. Heinsbergen executed the luxurious stylized artwork reflecting the Southern California lifestyle of sunshine, waves, and lush foliage. Heinsbergen was born in Holland in 1894 and immigrated to Los Angeles in 1905. After studying at the Chouinard Institute in Los Angeles, he formed his own company, the A. T. Heinsbergen Company, and created murals still found in the Hollywood Pantages, the Biltmore Hotel, and Los Angeles City Hall, among other buildings. Late in his life, when Heinsbergen was asked about the impending extinction of the grand movie palace, he said, "You know what really killed them? No parking. People started going to the suburban theatres so they could park their cars. It's as simple as that." Anthony's son, Tony Heinsbergen, worked with Brenda Levin on the restoration of his father's artwork.

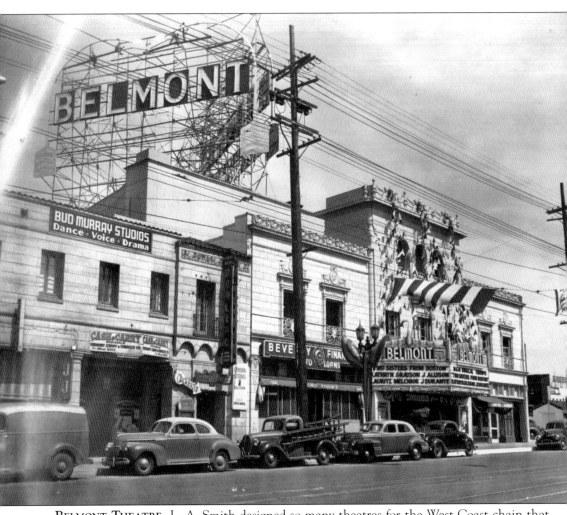

BELMONT THEATRE. L. A. Smith designed so many theatres for the West Coast chain that his initials should have stood for Los Angeles rather than Lewis. Built in 1926 with a modern ventilating system that provided a complete change of air every two minutes, the 1,300-seat theatre at 126 South Vermont Avenue was home to a Wurlitzer organ that could rival a 150-piece symphony orchestra. Ten months later, new management turned it into a legitimate theatre in which audiences preferred ushers dressed as girls rather than boys. When half its usherettes were dressed in lavender velvet girlish costumes, and the other half in flannel trousers and coats, the poll ran 6-1 in favor of feminine frocks. Today it would probably run to jeans and sweats at the mini-mall now on the site. Thanks to Milt Larsen, the massive gold-leaf panels and 30-foot columns representing the Four Graces were given new life, decorating the Mayfair Music Hall in Santa Monica, which was boarded up following the Northridge earthquake.

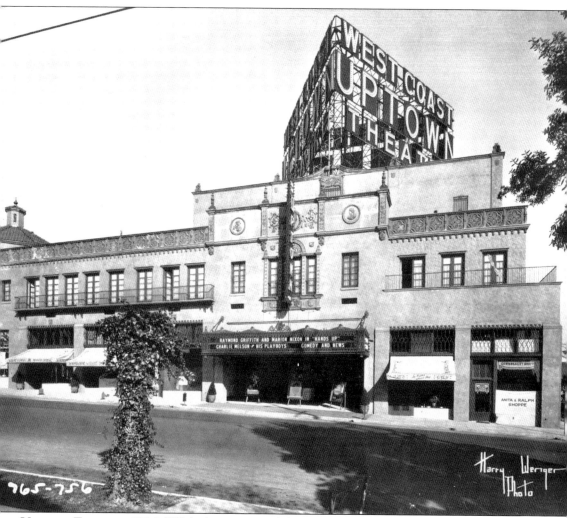

UPTOWN THEATRE, 1926. "With the opening of the Uptown Theatre," Sol Lesser declared in 1925, "the largest electric sign west of New York will be put into use. This sign will cover the top of the building. It will be forty feet high and eighty-five feet wide. The people of Los Angeles will be able to see this sign for miles around the theatre." The theatre under the sign blended Spanish and Italian renaissance as designed by architect L. A. Smith. Located at Western Avenue and Tenth Street (now Olympic Boulevard), it was sited away from the street to allow for an ample sidewalk for future street widening. In 1964, the theatre was replaced by a Ralph's supermarket.

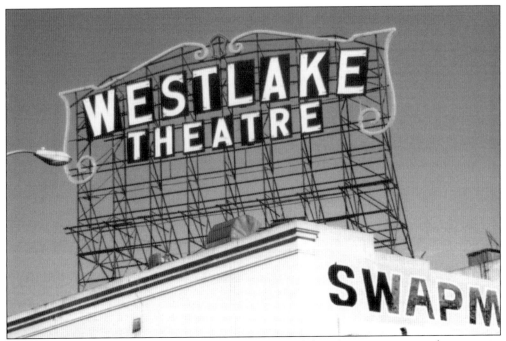

WESTLAKE THEATRE. Rather dingy in 1997, the Westlake Theatre was more glamorous in September 1926 when it opened with a splashy premiere of Warner Brothers' *Other Women's Husbands*. Designed by Richard M. Bates at 636 South Alvarado Street, the Westlake is in the Spanish baroque style. Although it is now atop a swap meet, the large restored neon sign is a historical and cultural monument, still attracting people from miles around.

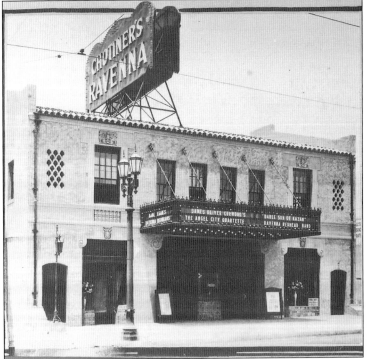

RAVENNA THEATRE, 1926. Richard D. King designed theatres for the Chotiner chain, including the 1925 Ravenna, formerly on Vermont Avenue south of Beverly Boulevard. Max Chotiner married Alice Calhoun, whom he met at one of his theatres, in 1926. They remarried in 1948, requesting the judge (unfortunately unavailable) who had pronounced their 1938 divorce final. Upon his wife's death in 1966, Chotiner endowed a research wing at City of Hope in her honor.

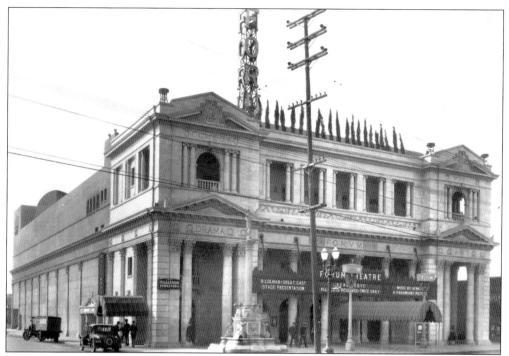

FORUM THEATRE, 1926. A 1922 headline in the *Los Angeles Times* announced, "Playhouse to be Built Away From Congested District." After all, the city limits had only been pushed out from Western Avenue a scant few decades earlier, so when Edward J. Borgmeyer designed the Forum Theatre—4050 West Pico Boulevard, just east of Crenshaw Boulevard—in the grand style of ancient Rome, it was far from the center of the city.

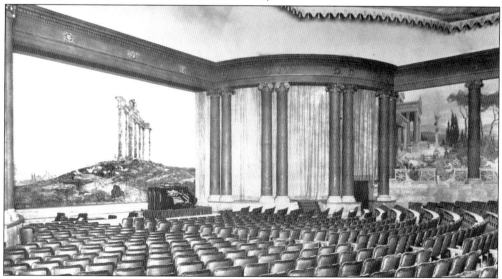

FORUM THEATRE, 1924. The theatre opened to huge crowds in 1924 with D. W. Griffith's *America*, attracting movie stars, mothers' groups, and patriotic organizations galore. The titanic pipe organ by W. W. Kimball Company required five freight cars to transport thousands of pipes from Chicago. It moved across town to the Wiltern in 1933. Borgmeyer's vision of antiquity has fared well. The Forum's columns now create a spectacular entrance to a church.

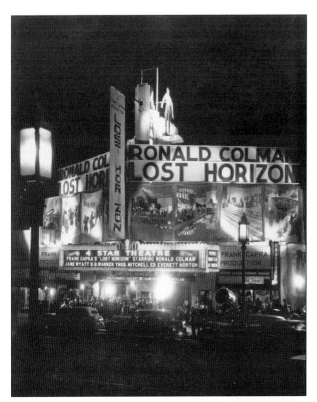

FOUR STAR THEATRE, 1937.
Movies have been an escape since their beginning, and the March 1937 premiere *of Lost Horizon* was no exception. Designed by Clifford A. Balch, the Four Star at 5112 Wilshire Boulevard was the perfect Art Deco setting to contemplate utopia—or at least to escape the Depression for two hours. It is now used for a different type of contemplation; it is a church.

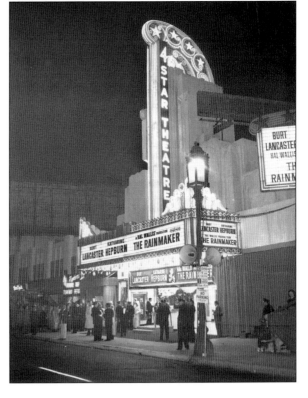

FOUR STAR THEATRE, 1956. Events are rarely planned in the hope of a rainy evening, but rumor has it that producer Hal B. Wallis checked with the weather bureau before Paramount chose December 18, 1956, as the premiere date for *The Rainmaker.* Luckily, a dry evening didn't dampen premiere-goers' spirits. The post-premiere party, held at the Ambassador Hotel, was a benefit for the City of Hope.

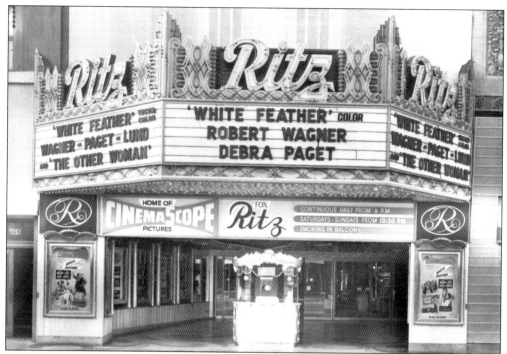

RITZ THEATRE, 1955. All theatres have stories, and the 1926 L. A. Smith–designed Ritz Theatre at 5214 Wilshire Boulevard had some that were quirkier than most. A 1949 "earthquake," for example, was strangely site-specific. Patrons panicked when the building started shaking . . . until the quake was traced to a horde of teenage boys pounding up and down the metal fire escape in a less-than-subtle attempt to sneak in without paying.

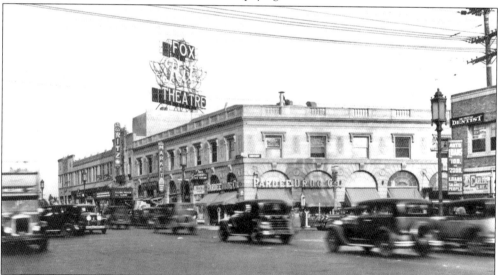

RITZ THEATRE, 1934. Another oddity was a 1933 lawsuit by a woman who was attacked by a lion. When the woman ventured close to his cage, the nasty beast stuck his head in a pail of milk and viciously sneezed on her. Less unusual was the final chapter. John Trayne wrote its eulogy: "L.A. already has a plethora of . . . parking lots. How about pulling some of them down and building theatres?"

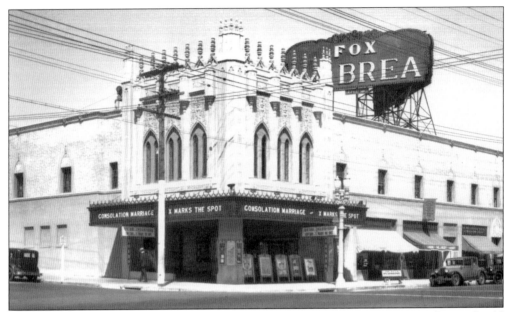

LA BREA THEATRE, 1932. The church that is comfortably ensconced in the La Brea Theatre should appreciate Richard D. King's design, which blends Moorish elements with Gothic windows. The 1926 plans included a radio tower rising over the roof like a steeple. Located at La Brea Avenue and Ninth Street, the building was the sixth theatre in the Chotiner Amusement chain.

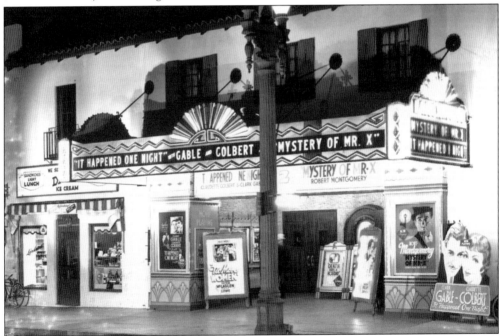

LARCHMONT THEATRE, 1934. Although the theatre at 149 North Larchmont Boulevard was built in 1921 for real estate investor J. J. La Bonte, he was quickly overshadowed by a celebrity owner. Alice Calhoun was a silent-film star, or, to quote Grace Kingsley, "The only girl picture star who owns a theatre . . . the Miss Midas of the movies . . . everything in a business way that Alice's dainty fingers have touched has turned to gold."

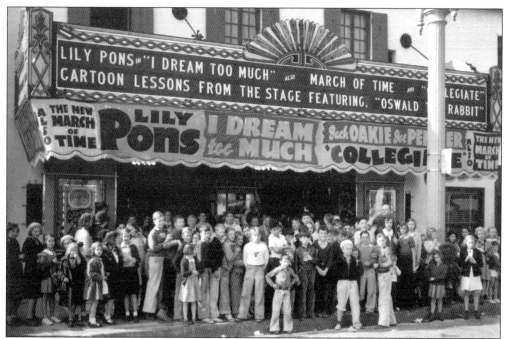

LARCHMONT THEATRE, 1935. A 1932 film party at the Larchmont was declared a howling success, and not one child was turned away. Scores of boys brought dogs that frolicked outside until their young masters returned. The video rental store now on the site doesn't have the same pizzazz nor does it carry any of Alice Calhoun's movies, not even the ironically titled *The Isle of Forgotten Women*.

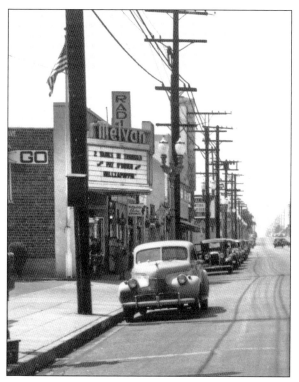

MELVAN THEATRE, 1941. The Melvan Theatre's claim on history came via an unusual route. Building permits for 5308 Melrose Avenue, now occupied by the Raleigh Studios administration building, leave dates and architects shadowy, but shortly after becoming an art house called the Encore in 1963, space was rented to the predominately gay Metropolitan Community Church. It was the forerunner of the first Christian denomination to affirm gay men and women as children of God.

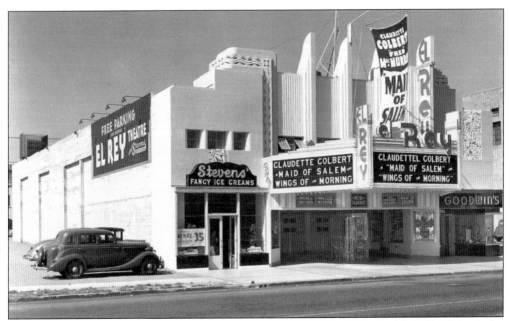

THE EL REY THEATRE, 1937. In the heart of the Miracle Mile at 5515 Wilshire Boulevard, the El Rey was a 900-seat first-run neighborhood theatre, originally opened by the Pacific States Theatre chain in June 1937. Designed by prolific theatre architect Clifford A. Balch in the Art Deco style, it is now a live-music venue. Many original elements remain, including the terrazzo sidewalk, box office, and some interior decoration.

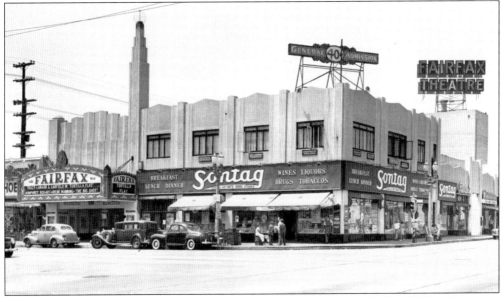

FAIRFAX THEATRE, 1943. Architect W. C. Pennell, who frequently worked with John C. Austin, designed mansions and churches in West Adams, apartments and business buildings downtown, and an ice-skating rink and a hospital, among other structures. He began work on the Fairfax Theatre in 1929. Originally a 1,500-seat, single-screen theatre, the buildings at 7907 Beverly Boulevard currently house a Regency triplex as well as shops along Beverly Boulevard and Fairfax Avenue.

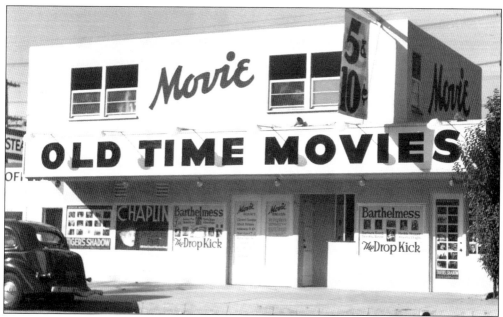

SILENT MOVIE THEATRE, 1945. "Talkies? They're against my religion—almost," said John Hampton, who with his wife, Dorothy, founded the Silent Movie Theatre at 611 North Fairfax Avenue in 1942. A later owner, Laurence Austin, welcomed audiences to the strains of *Pomp and Circumstance* until his death in the theatre at the hands of a gunman hired by his projectionist/lover. The tiny theatre is kept open by fans of early film.

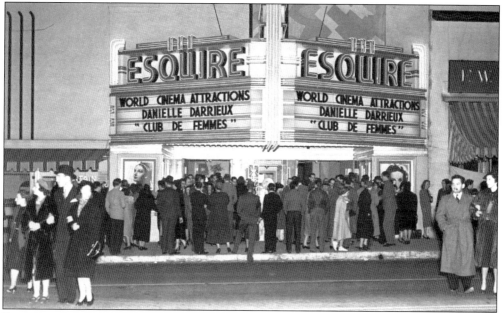

ESQUIRE THEATRE, 1946. It's rare for a theatre to be less famous than its replacement. The Esquire Theatre, 419 North Fairfax Avenue, was reputedly designed by Clifford A. Balch, probably in 1931. It showed foreign and art films from at least 1937 to 1953. What is indisputable is that looking up in Canter's, the most famous deli in Los Angeles, part of the theatre's original ceiling is still visible.

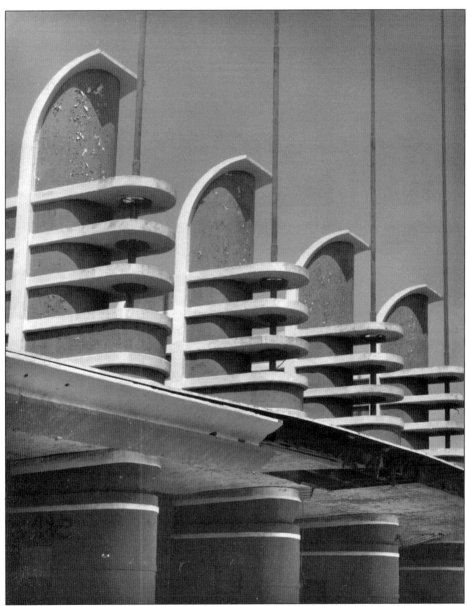

PAN PACIFIC AUDITORIUM. Shortly after dusk on an evening in May 1989, the Pan Pacific Auditorium erupted with flames shooting 200 feet into the sky. As smoke mushroomed over the city, firefighters from 50 companies fought to contain the blaze. But by 10:00 p.m., all that remained at 7600 West Beverly Boulevard were three charred walls. The landmark fin-shaped pylons at the entrance slowly crumbled to the ground. The distinctive, Streamline Moderne design by Plummer, Wurdeman, and Becket had been built in less than six weeks to house a 1935 home show, complete with two full-sized model homes. An ice rink was added later. Hedda Hopper enthused over the Ice Follies of 1939, before critiquing the celebrities testing the ice after the show. Joan Crawford's stricken look when her skates hit the ice was prominently mentioned, whereas Ronald Reagan was described as "okeh." The Pan Pacific played host to sporting events, music from Leopold Stokowski to Elvis, political gatherings, circuses, and trade shows. (Frank E. Cooper Jr.)

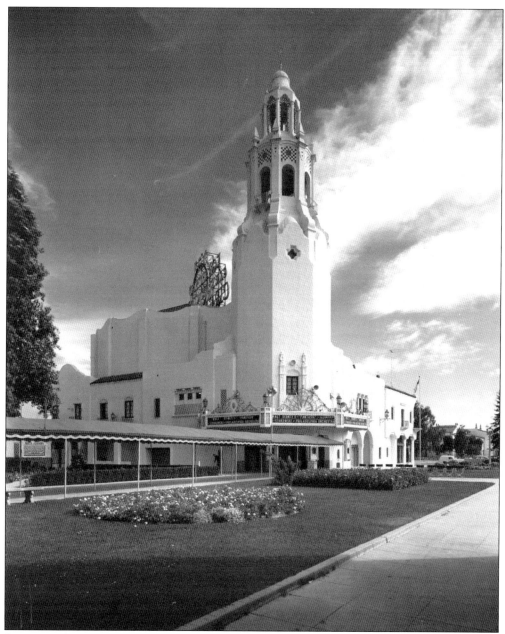

CARTHAY CIRCLE THEATRE, 1941. In one of the most significant losses to the city's historic theatre fabric, the Carthay Circle Theatre at 6316 San Vicente Boulevard fell to the bulldozers in 1969. Designed by architect Dwight Gibbs in the Spanish revival style and opened in 1926, its circular auditorium and 140-foot tower were unique. The interior was a tribute to the early years of California's history, featuring murals illustrating pioneer times by Frank Tenney Johnson and California impressionist Alson Skinner Clark. Johnson's love for the West was apparent, notably his depiction of the Donner Party on the Carthay's curtain. Clark studied in Chicago, New York, and Paris, but he made Pasadena his home in 1920. How ironic that a theatre that paid such lovely tribute to California's history would become a casualty of the city's lack of respect for its past.

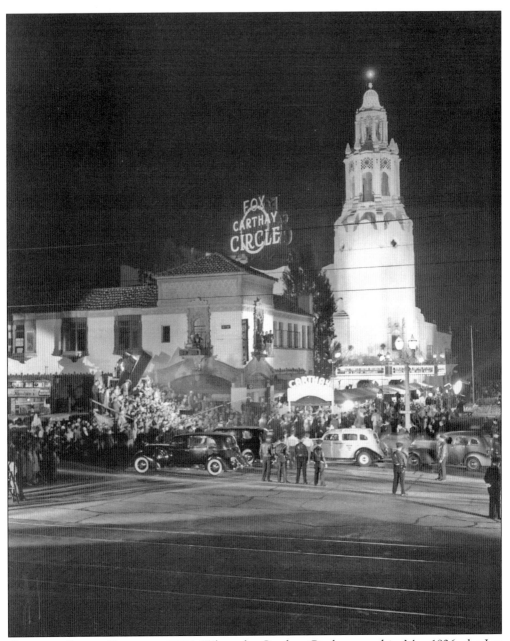

CARTHAY CIRCLE THEATRE, 1937. When the Carthay Circle opened in May 1926, the *Los Angeles Times* proclaimed it "The beacon light of amusement seekers"—and it was, but for only a short 43 years. The opening night, featuring Cecil B. DeMille's *The Volga Boatman*, was the first of many film premieres at this glamorous theatre. The June 1937 opening of *Wee Willie Winkie*, starring Shirley Temple, was the first time the studio held a premiere for one of the child star's films. Having already starred in dozens of movies by the ripe old age of nine, she had certainly earned it. One highlight of the event was the showing of color pictures of the recent coronation of England's George VI. Even though it had already officially "premiered" in Atlanta and New York, probably the most famous opening at this location was the West Coast gala premiere of *Gone with the Wind* in 1939.

Three

HOLLYWOOD

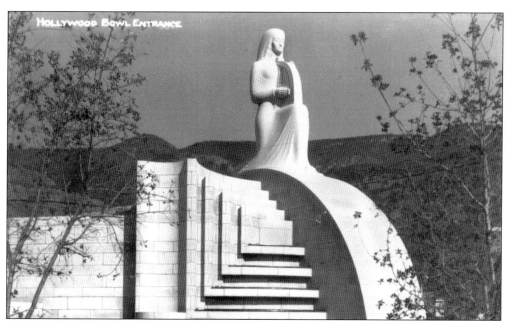

HOLLYWOOD BOWL, MUSE OF MUSIC. Nothing says stars like the Hollywood Bowl . . . except maybe the Oscar. Sculptor George Stanley had a hand in both: He molded the Oscar statuette in 1927 from a cocktail napkin sketch by Cedric Gibbons, and his *Muse of Music* greets visitors at the entrance to the Hollywood Bowl. The fountain was sculpted in 1939 under the auspices of the Works Progress Administration, Hollywood Bowl Association, and the Los Angeles County Board of Supervisors. Carved from granite quarried near Victorville, the *Muse* and her smaller sisters, *Dance* and *Drama*, survived years of neglect before a 2006 restoration. Beginning as a simple stage in 1922, the bowl gained its iconic design of concentric circles in later years. Allied Architects' first shell in 1926 began the acoustical problems that have plagued successive generations of architects from Lloyd Wright to Frank Gehry. Remedies have tweaked or totally redesigned the shell. Its latest rebuild was in 2004. (Los Angeles Photo Postcard.)

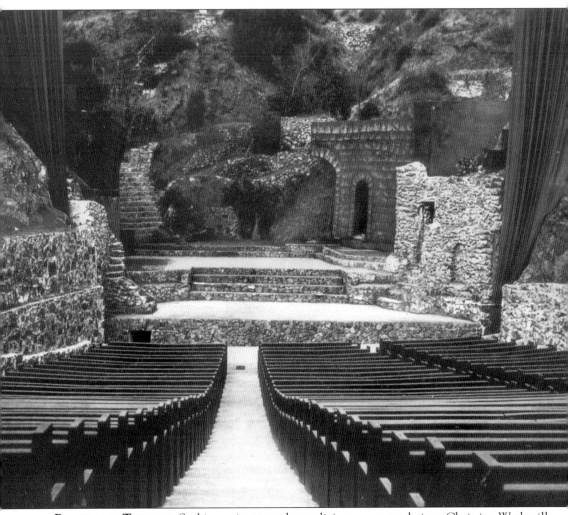

PILGRIMAGE THEATRE. Seeking a site to produce religious pageants, heiress Christine Wetherill Stevenson helped form the Theatre Arts Alliance. The organization bought land in the Cahuenga Pass to build an outdoor theatre. After organizational dissension over design and her focus on religious productions, Stevenson was bought out. Not to be deterred from her dream, she and society matron Mrs. Chauncey D. Clark purchased a nearby 45-acre parcel in 1920 for an outdoor amphitheatre. With brief interruptions because of fire and war, Stevenson's original *Pilgrimage Play* was produced annually from 1920 to 1964. This wood structure was destroyed by a brush fire in 1929 and rebuilt in concrete two years later by the WPA, designed to resemble the Jerusalem Gates. Located at 2580 Cahuenga Boulevard, it was renamed the John Anson Ford Theatre in 1976. The Theatre Arts Alliance was reorganized into another group that opened a rival outdoor theatre in 1922: the Hollywood Bowl. (Postcard uncredited.)

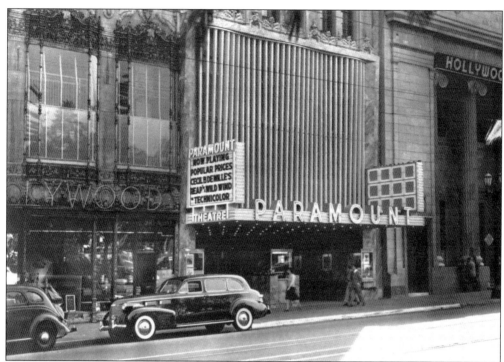

PARAMOUNT THEATRE, 1942. Now the El Capitan, the Paramount Theatre began its life in 1926 as a legitimate theatre at 6838 Hollywood Boulevard. Its premiere production was *Charlot's Revue*, starring Gertrude Lawrence and Bea Lillie. Morgan, Walls and Clements designed the Spanish baroque–revival exterior, and G. Albert Lansburgh its East Indian–revival interior.

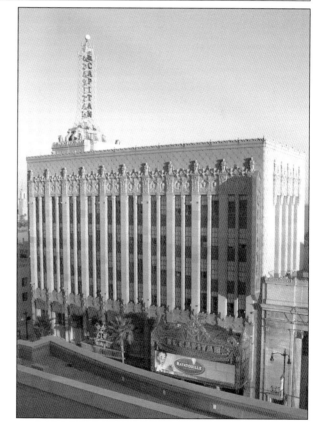

EL CAPITAN. Beginning in the late 1980s, the El Capitan has been painstakingly restored and maintained. In 1941, it hosted the premiere of the landmark film *Citizen Kane*. Now operated by the Walt Disney Company, the "El Cap" exclusively shows first-run Disney films, usually incorporating child-oriented live entertainment—coming full circle from a time when theatres always had a show before the film started. (Frank E. Cooper Jr.)

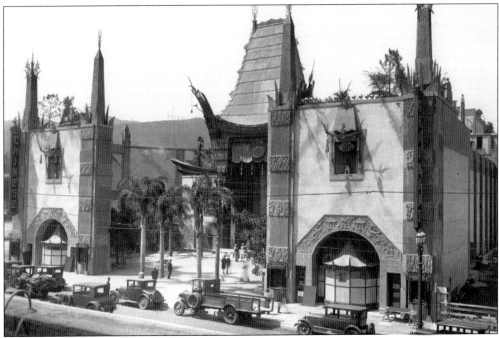

GRAUMAN'S CHINESE THEATRE, 1927. The most famous movie theatre in the world, Grauman's Chinese at 6925 Hollywood Boulevard opened on May 18, 1927, with a premiere of Cecil B. DeMille's *King of Kings*. Designed by Meyer and Holler, the dazzling theatre featured antiques imported from China and an exotic Chinese pagoda–style design.

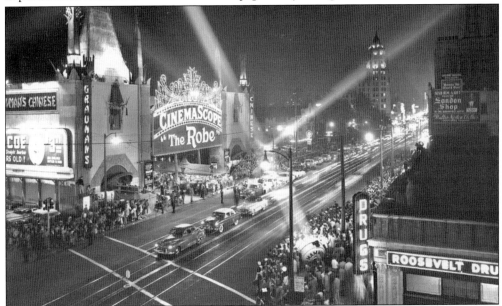

GRAUMAN'S CHINESE THEATRE, 1953. Another movie tradition bequeathed by Sid Grauman—the dazzling, show-stopping premiere with klieg lights sweeping the night sky over the Chinese— began on opening night in May 1927 and continues to this day. For the premiere of *The Robe* in September 1953, the theatre was remodeled at a cost of $100,000 to add Cinemascope technology and to reconfigure the seating.

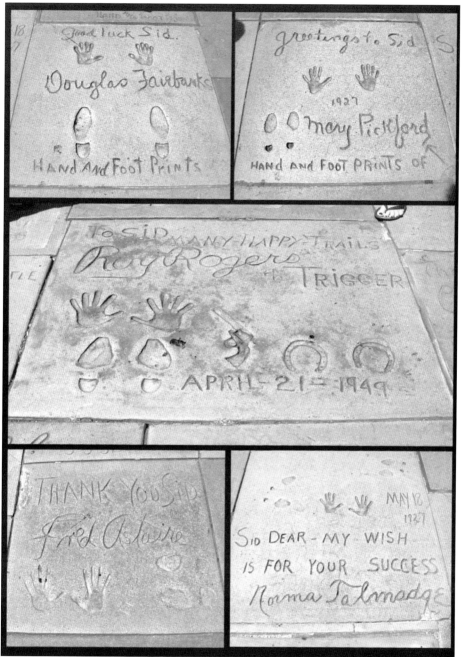

GRAUMAN'S CHINESE THEATRE FORECOURT HAND AND FOOTPRINTS. One of the "Only in Hollywood" traditions for which Grauman's Chinese is known—the footprints in cement of the forecourt—began in April 1927. The first to be immortalized were Norma Talmadge, Mary Pickford, Douglas Fairbanks, and Sid Grauman himself. Rumor claimed the cement was of a special formula locked in a safe. Some stars' slabs included identifying features, such as Harpo Marx's harp, Sonja Henie's ice skates, John Barrymore's profile, Harold Lloyd's glasses and even Roy Rogers's horse, Trigger's, hoof prints. Stars prints are added to this day, making new generations part of Hollywood history. (Frank E. Cooper Jr.)

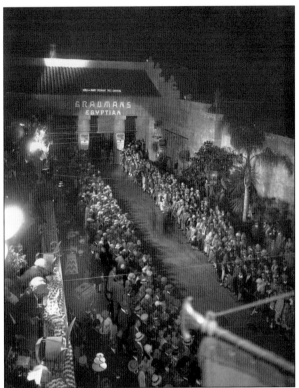

GRAUMAN'S EGYPTIAN THEATRE PREMIERE, 1926. Mary Pickford and Douglas Fairbanks weren't able to attend their dual premiere of *Sparrows* and *The Black Pirate* in 1926, but that didn't stop Sid Grauman from turning the event into a star-studded extravaganza. Designed by Meyer and Holler in 1922 at 6712 Hollywood Boulevard, this cinema gem was renovated in 1998 and is now operated by the American Cinematheque.

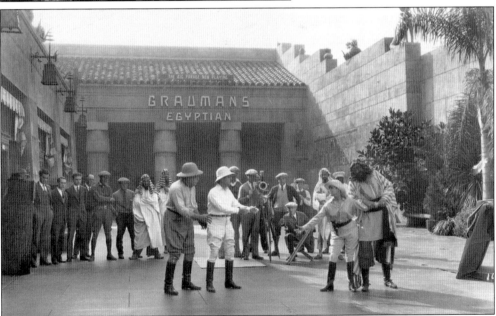

GRAUMAN'S EGYPTIAN THEATRE COURTYARD, 1927. Not every film was memorable, but some did tie in nicely to the theatre's theme. Neely Edwards conceived a new dance called "Hollywood Mummy" for the film *Mummy Love*. He commented, "Now that practically every city has been honored by a different phase of jazzmania . . . Hollywood should also attain a niche." It wasn't the next Charleston. Producer Joe Rock is better remembered for Stan Laurel comedies.

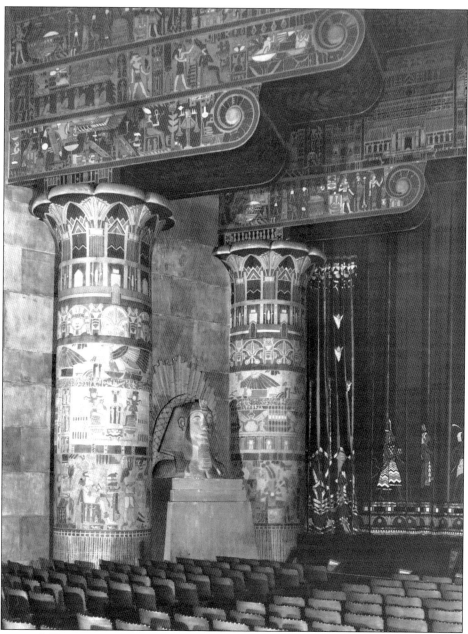

GRAUMAN'S EGYPTIAN THEATRE INTERIOR, 1923. Work on Grauman's downtown Metropolitan Theatre began before the Egyptian, but the latter opened several months earlier, on October 18, 1922. To celebrate the opening, Grauman produced another gala premiere, presenting Douglas Fairbanks's *Robin Hood*. This was Grauman's first foray out of downtown and into Hollywood. He created a showplace like none other, replete with hieroglyphics and graceful capitals topping columns shaped like lotus blossoms. After opening night, critic Edwin Schallert wrote, "The sphinxes that adorn the proscenium imply that silence is the tribute of appreciation for the visual drama. The Egyptian inscriptions perhaps suggest that mystic incantation of light which gives life to the shadowed surface of the silver sheet." The screen drama surely paled in comparison to the stimulating interior.

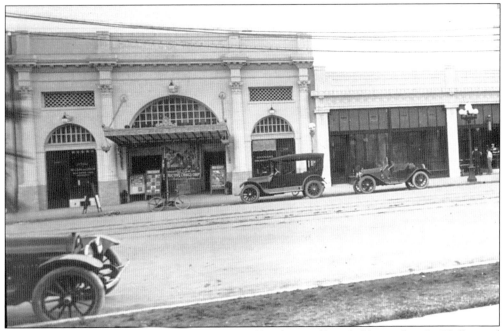

HOLLYWOOD THEATRE, 1916. One for the record books—well, probably not, but the Hollywood Theatre at 6764 Hollywood Boulevard was an early film house, designed in 1913 by Kremple and Erkes. It was damaged by arson in 1933. Captain Wolfe, a fire department spokesperson, pointed out that the theatre had been the site of stink bombings "and from all indications the persons responsible for these depredations caused the fire."

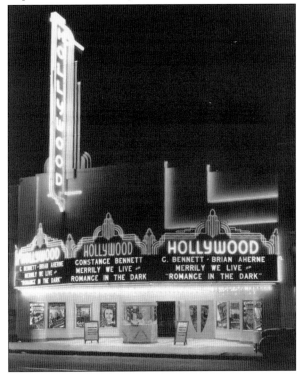

HOLLYWOOD THEATRE, 1938. The remodeling in 1938 was a double-hitter, with Clifford A. Balch making changes and a new electrical sign being added a few months later. S. Charles Lee reputedly lent a hand at one point, but his name doesn't show up on any building permits. The marquee is intact but it now fronts the Guinness Book of World Records Museum.

VOGUE THEATRE, 1935. In July 1935, the Vogue Theater, designed by S. Charles Lee, opened with a double bill that would seem prophetic: *The Phantom Fiend*, aka "*The Lodger*," and *Ladies Crave Excitement*. Ghost-hunters claim that the theatre has several spirits, including a spectral projectionist capable of changing a film reel. The theatre at 6675 Hollywood Boulevard has been empty (except for the ghosts) for years. Its future is currently unknown.

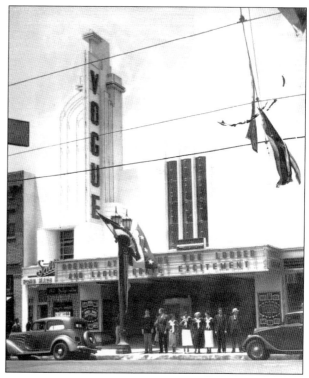

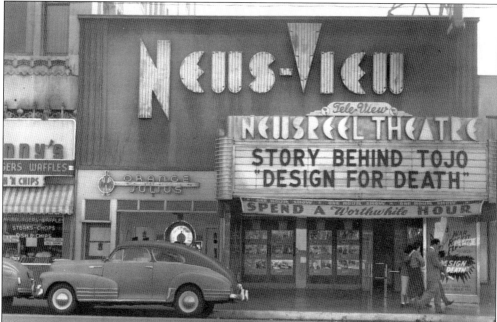

NEWS-VIEW THEATRE, 1944. Some theatres thrived on disaster. Before the six o'clock news invaded every household, footage of breaking news—wars, riot, typhoons—was the province of theatres like the News-View, at 6656 Hollywood Boulevard. Opened in 1940, newsreels were air-expressed from New York in only 15 hours or from London in 40. Post-TV, the theatre by S. Tilden Norton and Frederick Wallis showed pornography before becoming a church.

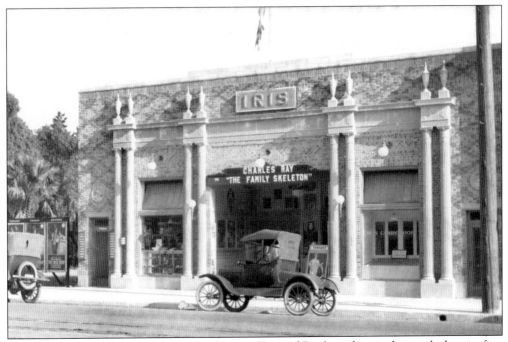

IRIS THEATRE, 1918. It's hard to believe that Hollywood Boulevard was a dirt road when its first theatre was built. The Iris Theatre doesn't look like the forerunner of grand movie palaces, and the bare ground gives no clue that it would someday be covered with stars—nor that C. A. Balch would remodel the theatre to an Art Deco style in 1934.

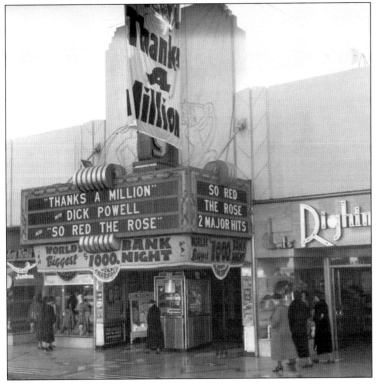

IRIS THEATRE, 1936. When Carol Burnett was a teenager making 75¢ an hour as a cashier at the Iris Theatre at Hollywood Boulevard and Wilcox Avenue, she probably didn't care who had redesigned her workplace. The theatre was remodeled again in 1955, reputedly by S. Charles Lee, and apparently once more within two decades. More changes are coming. At press time, the shell wore an application to sell alcoholic beverages.

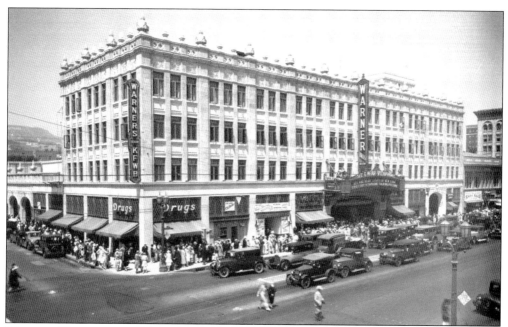

WARNER THEATRE 1928 (AKA "WARNER PACIFIC"). The four-story Italianate Beaux-Arts style theatre at 6433 Hollywood Boulevard was designed by G. Albert Lansburgh. To celebrate the ground breaking in January 1926, a local competitor dispatched a hearse followed by two "mourners" to the ceremonies. The sign on the hearse offered the dubious compliment, "Success to Warner Brothers, Sid Grauman."

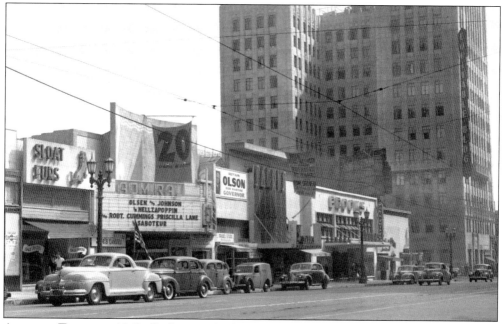

ADMIRAL THEATRE, 1943. On January 2, 1940, at 9:00 a.m., the first legal moment of the New Year, a contract was signed designating S. Charles Lee as the architect for the Admiral Theatre at 6321 Hollywood Boulevard, on land owned by the Stern Film Corporation since at least 1927. It became the Vine Theatre in 1968 and is still in existence today.

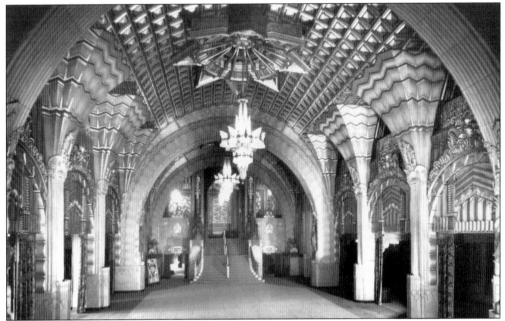

PANTAGES LOBBY, 1930. Critic Edwin Schallert wrote after the gala 1930 opening, "The Pantages Theatre is a step beyond any other theatre that has been opened here in its note of modernity. Indeed. Architecture seems to have progressed to new moods since the last playhouse made its debut." The lobby is an Art Deco interpretation of an ancient barrel-vaulted ceiling with movie motifs never imagined by its Roman forbearers.

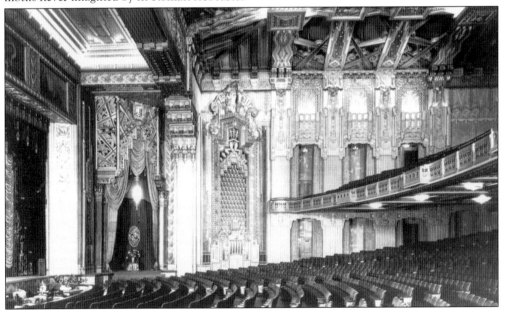

PANTAGES AUDITORIUM, 1930. Although B. Marcus Priteca was well known for designing sumptuously beautiful theatres, he was so successful because he also excelled at creating good sightlines and crystal clear acoustics. He once said, "Seeing is hearing." He knew that using all of the senses enhanced the film-going experience. The dramatic and dazzling interior was refurbished in 2000 and is now a live theatre venue.

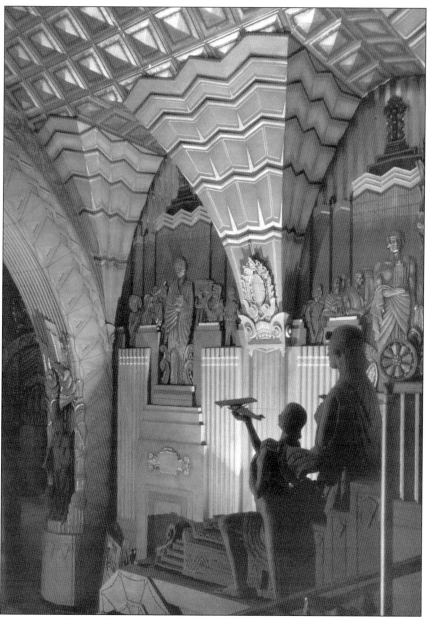

PANTAGES DETAIL. The 1929 masterpiece at 6233 Hollywood Boulevard was Alexander Pantages's last theatre before a sex scandal ruined him financially and his chain was sold to RKO. The opening program included *Floradora Girl*, starring Marion Davies, a Mickey Mouse cartoon, and a Fanchon and Marco revue, and "an enticingly proffered" trapeze finish, part of an act that Schallert went on to say was "more elaborately staged than any of their familiar divertissements and is a triumph of costuming . . . the audience also responded to the work of 'Slim' Martin and his jazz band, but after all, what can equal a Walt Disney cartoon?" The premiere had everything except Alexander Pantages. He was in jail, charged with the statutory rape of an underage showgirl. Efforts to have the showman released for the premiere failed, and Pantages listened to the music, songs, and applause through a radio system in the jail physician's office. (Courtesy of J. Eric Lynxwiler.)

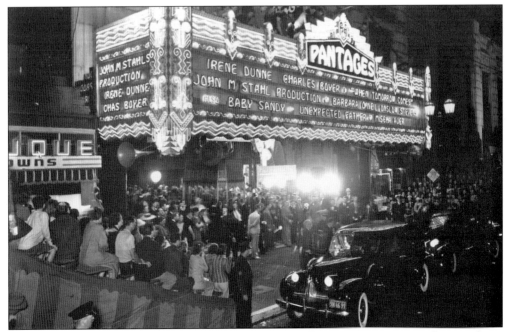

PANTAGES PREMIERE. At the August 1939 premiere of *When Tomorrow Comes,* the crowd was estimated to be 5,000—and that was just regular folk. It didn't include the multitude of stars who attended. While Douglas Fairbanks Jr., Jack Benny, Lucille Ball, and Edgar Bergen walked the red carpet, the ungrateful crowd was disappointed because Mae West and W. C. Fields were expected but didn't show.

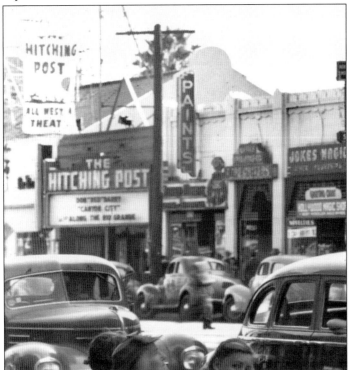

HITCHING POST THEATRE, 1944. Imagine a whole chain of theatres devoted exclusively to Westerns laden with shootin', gallopin,' and 10-gallon hats. The first Hitching Post opened in 1941 at 6262 Hollywood Boulevard, lightheartedly described by Lee Shippey as "what many persons think the center of a sink of immorality," hardly befittin' the silver screen's "plumb noble" heroes. Do ex-cowboys dream of their horses at the Metrolink station there now?

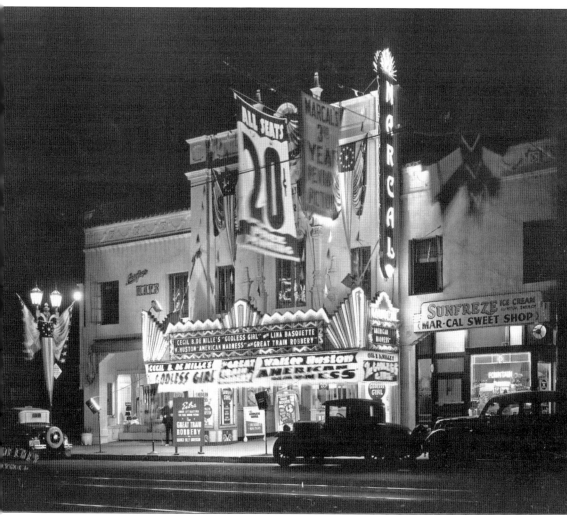

MARCAL THEATRE, 1937. Silent-film star and principal stockholder Alice Calhoun drove a bulldozer when ground was broken for Hansen Theaters' new Marcal Theatre, designed by William E. Young, at 6021–6025 Hollywood Boulevard in 1925. Through several decades, the theatre made headlines with charitable benefits. Owner Mark Hansen, however, accrued different press notices. His name was stamped in gold on the Black Dahlia's "little brown book." In 1949, a blonde taxi dancer claimed she showed Hansen two nude photos of herself before disrobing and going into a bedroom with him. When he "began to shave with an electric razor," said the *Los Angeles Times,* "she decided it would be a good time to shoot him." He survived. She was convicted but later committed after a suicide attempt and several hysterical scenes, including a strip tease in the Hall of Justice. The Marcal was demolished. What looks like a theatre next door are the remnants of a market designed by Gordon B. Kaufman in 1937 that became a pornography theatre in the 1970s.

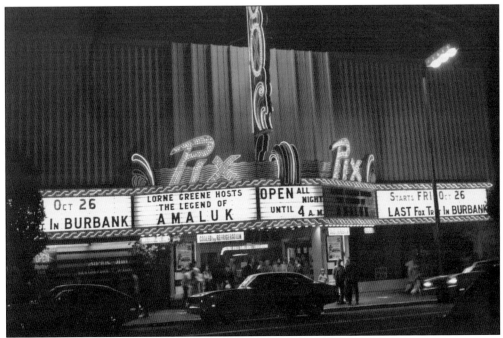

PIX THEATRE, 1967. A huge girder missed its chance for stardom in 1926 when the city foiled plans to film its journey to 6126 Hollywood Boulevard during daylight hours, but Morgan, Walls and Clements' design gave it a best supporting role in the balcony of Carter De Haven's Music Box Theatre anyway. From stage to screen and back, the theatre, once named the Pix, is now the Henry Fonda Playhouse.

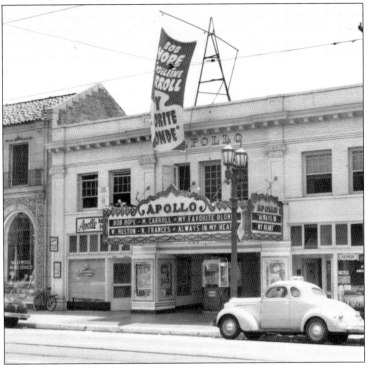

APOLLO THEATRE, 1942. The Apollo Theatre, by C. S. Albright, opened its doors at 5544 Hollywood Boulevard in 1921, with a showing of *Nineteen and Phyllis*. The manager voted to ban Fatty Arbuckle's films from California theatres, following accusations that Arbuckle caused the death of starlet Virginia Rappe. The retail space that replaced the theatre is as forgettable as its first film, but the graffiti adorning it is certainly a scandal.

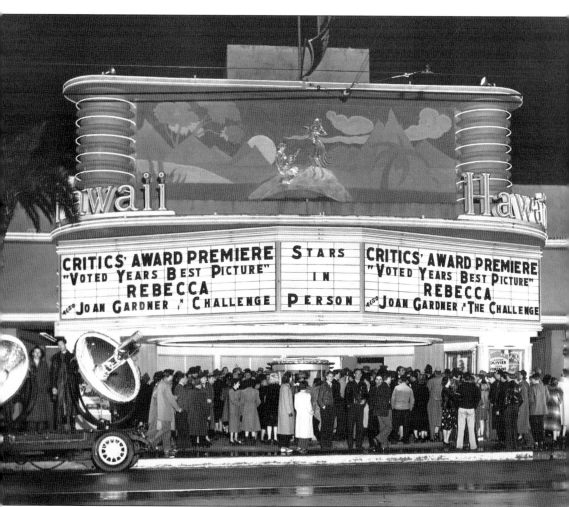

HAWAII THEATRE, 1940. Whatever else one may say about Albert Galston and Jay Sutton, they were consummate showmen. When the Hawaii Theatre, designed by Carl G. Moeller with Clarence J. Smale, opened at 5941 Hollywood Boulevard in 1940, it had already received miles of press about the black-light tropical murals, ample parking, and comfortable rocking seats. Harold Lloyd was on hand when the theatre floor was poured and left his famous round spectacles embedded in the concrete. Galston recalled some later publicity stunts for their mostly B movies. For *Cat People* in 1942, the box office was converted into the head of an immense cat, with tickets sold through its mouth. This was topped by a patron during the run of *The Bat Whispers*. Getting too much into the spirit, he released a bagful of live bats that took the theatre weeks to remove. The Salvation Army moved into the theatre in 1964.

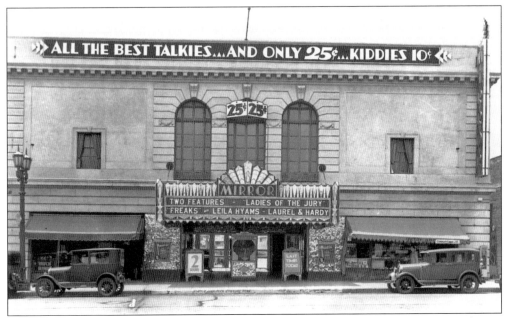

MIRROR THEATRE, 1933. Given the traditional superstitions of show business, covering a theatre in broken mirrors seems like a dicey proposition. Maybe it was: The idea only lasted from 1931 to 1935. The mosaic of mirrors was supposed to be aligned in such a way that it would not reflect glare. No doubt the opening night audience loved *Sin Takes a Holiday* unless glare-proof glass deflects criticism, too.

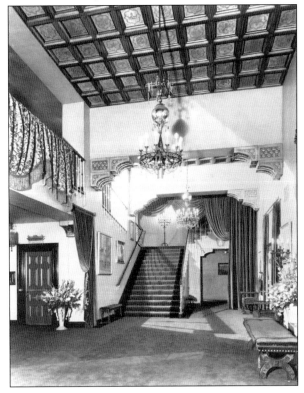

MIRROR THEATRE. The Italianate building designed by Myron Hunt and H. C. Chambers at 1615 North Vine Street has changed names nearly as often as fashionable ladies have changed hem lengths. Sometimes showing movies, sometimes legitimate theatre, it was born the Vine-Street in 1927, but other names include the Mirror, the Studio, CBS Radio Playhouse, Huntington Hartford, and James A. Doolittle. It is now the namesake of actor Ricardo Montalban.

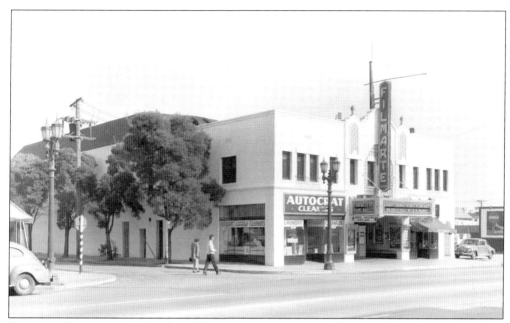

FILMARTE THEATRE, 1946. Alma Whitaker's gossip column, "Sugar and Spie" was quite taken with the Filmarte's opening crowd who she described as "different . . . evening-clothed sophisticates and arty-looking men with red sweaters under coats, very Bohemian." Hollywood's first art house, at 1228 North Vine Street, was opened in 1928, screening foreign films, art films, and even old silents. The lounge served coffee and cigarettes. News in Pictures was also offered, as "after all, things keep on happening in spite of art."

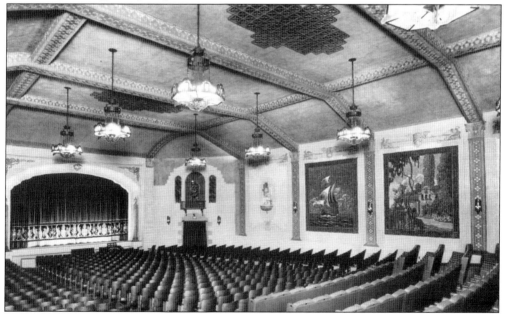

FILMARTE THEATRE INTERIOR, 1927. Whitaker was also fond of the manager, whom she described as capable and "piquantly feminine." She commented that Regge Doran had "lost seven pounds working and planning for that opening and she only weighed 100 in the first place." In 1952, the now-vanished theatre, then named for Steve Allen, was used for television production.

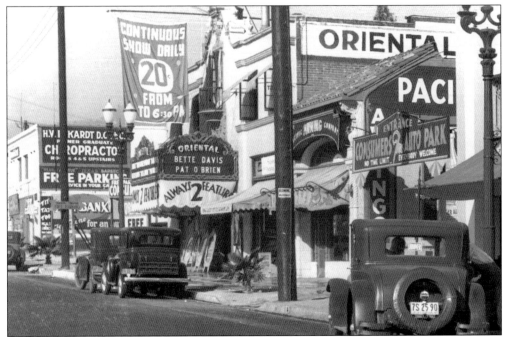

Oriental Theatre, 1932. It is rather like a Hollywood story: a nice Spanish-style theatre with an excellent pedigree, in this case a Meyer and Holler design c. 1921, changed its name from the Granada to the Oriental in the 1930s or 1940s, most likely in a quest for exoticism. And now? The former theatre at 7425 Sunset Boulevard is making a stab at music stardom as the Guitar Center.

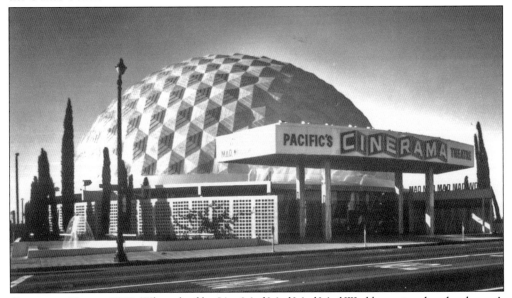

Cinerama Dome, 1963. When the film *It's a Mad Mad Mad Mad World* premiered at the theatre's opening in 1963, moviegoers must have thought just that when they first saw this concrete geodesic dome. Designed by Welton Becket, the Cinerama Dome is constructed of 316 concrete hexagonal panels. Located in the heart of Hollywood at 6360 Sunset Boulevard, this Los Angeles cultural monument was restored in 2004.

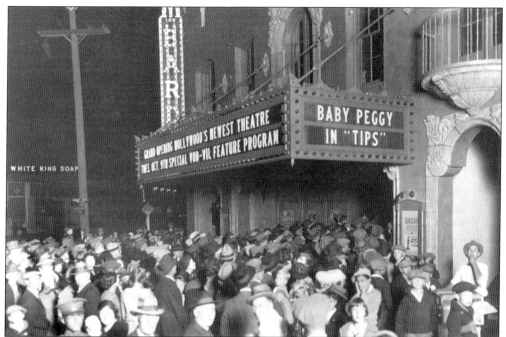

BARD'S HOLLYWOOD THEATRE, 1923. Colossal Babylonion sets for D. W. Griffith's 1916 film *Intolerance* were removed from 4473 Sunset Drive around 1921 to clear the way for Bard's new theatre. Baby Peggy appeared to promote her comedy "Tips" at the grand opening in 1923, an evening of short films and vaudeville. Baby Peggy made more than 150 two-reel comedies before committing the ultimate Hollywood crime of maturing into adulthood.

VISTA THEATRE, 1952. Renamed the Vista in the late 1920s, Bard's Hollywood was designed by L. A. Smith with a Spanish-style exterior and an Egyptian-influenced interior. Louis Bard operated several theatres in the Los Angeles area. In 1925, he partnered with Fred Miller, forming Far West Theatres and bringing such treasured properties as the Carthay Circle and Figueroa into their joint ownership. The Vista remains open and currently shows first-run films.

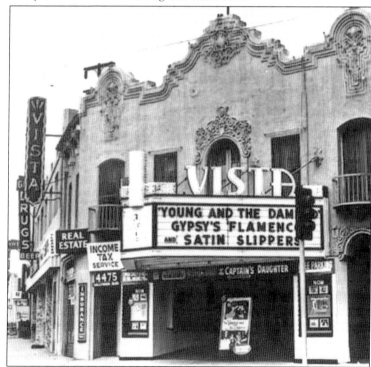

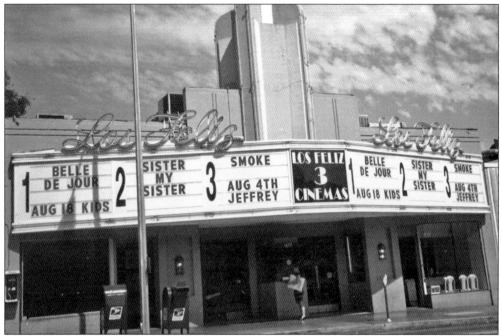

LOS FELIZ THEATRE, 1995. Now a triplex emblazoned with purple neon, "at first, this was in 1947, the Los Feliz was a neighborhood theatre," said Max Laemmle, who turned 1822–1826 North Vermont Boulevard into a well-respected art house. "Once in a while I'd book a good foreign film to fill a hole, rather than bring in a poor Hollywood film . . . now we only book foreign films."

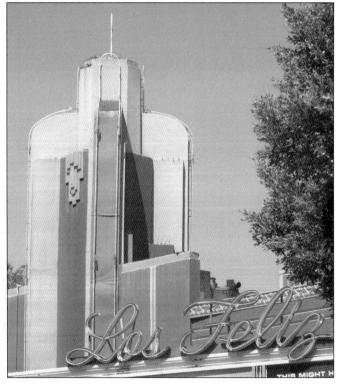

LOS FELIZ THEATRE. Before it was an art house, a letter writer reminisced about matinees costing a nickel for "Bugs Bunny Club" members, and believed the Los Feliz was the first movie house sensible enough to outlaw chewing gum. Earlier still, Howard Hughes and Harold Franklin joined forces to create a new theatre circuit; a 1934 building permit named Clifford A. Balch as architect for their Los Feliz theatre. (Frank E. Cooper Jr.)

Four

WESTSIDE

FOX WILSHIRE THEATRE, 1930. The September 19, 1930, gala opening of the theatre and premiere of the Marx Brothers' *Animal Crackers* created a confluence of local Beverly Hills civic leaders and Hollywood's elite. Groucho Marx once said, "Politics is the art of looking for trouble, finding it everywhere, diagnosing it incorrectly, and applying the wrong remedies." The mischief the Marx Brothers got up to while mingling with the politicians at this premiere wasn't reported. This was architect S. Charles Lee's second Los Angeles area building and theatre project. Originally built for the Fox Film Corporation at 8440 Wilshire Boulevard in Beverly Hills, the lavish Art Deco design went from the first floor to the top, including a fabulous Deco penthouse built for the chain's vice president, Howard Sheehan. Now the Wilshire Theatre, it hosts live performances and religious services.

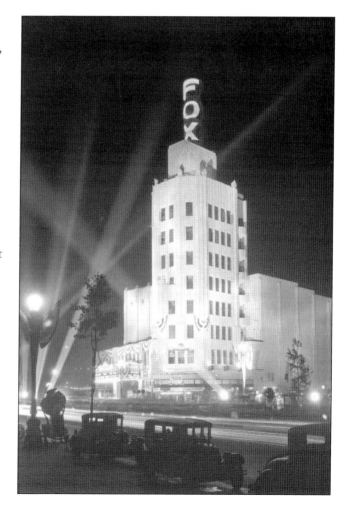

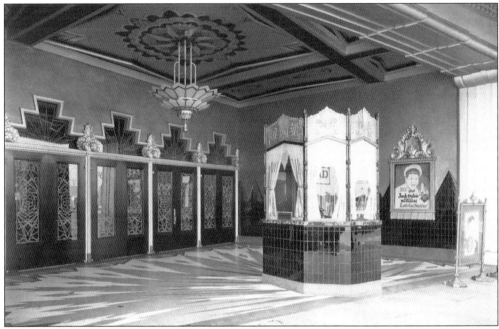

FOX WILSHIRE BOX OFFICE, 1930. Lee's box offices were not merely functional; they were also quite beautiful. When patrons stepped up to buy tickets, the magnificence assured them that they would be in for a treat. This was just the beginning, as their steps took them over a terrazzo sunburst to the ziggurat-topped doors that ushered them into the theatre.

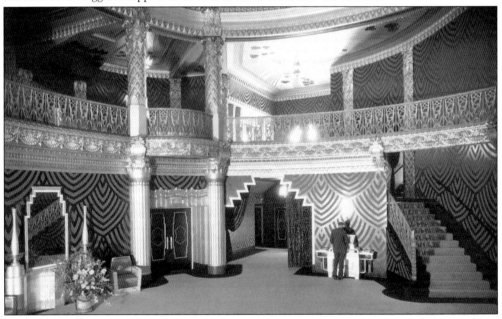

FOX WILSHIRE LOBBY, 1930. A movie palace if there ever was one, the Fox Wilshire could be viewed as a transitional design for Lee. While stylistically quite different from the Tower Theatre, he used the same elaborate embellishment, this time substituting modern, geometric, abstract designs for period revival motifs. During the 1930s, he would simplify his style even further by using the Streamline Moderne style.

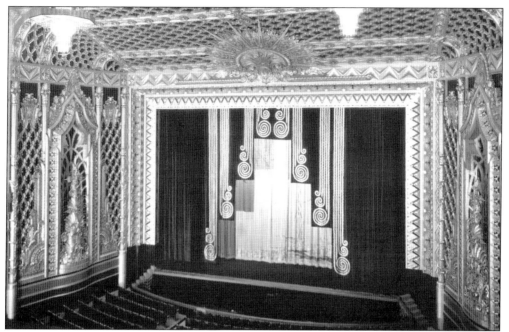

FOX WILSHIRE PROSCENIUM, 1930. This sumptuous Art Deco dream, dramatic in silver, black, and coral, was built as a first-run movie house, with additional facilities for live theatre. Since it differed significantly from the traditional designs used in vaudeville theatres, the use of the Art Deco style for the talking-picture house was a visual way to announce to patrons to prepare for a new experience.

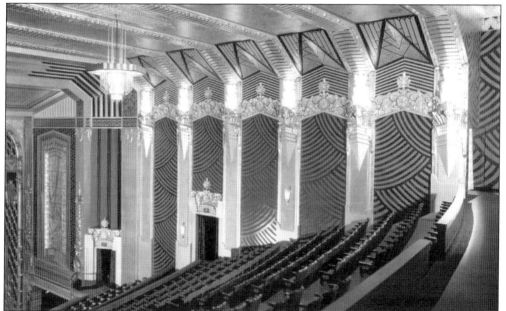

FOX WILSHIRE AUDITORIUM, 1930. An advertising brochure produced for the theatre stated, "A striking house in black and silver designed for neighborhood patronage." That seems like quite the understatement, but with Beverly Hills as the neighborhood, this glamorous auditorium is right at home. This theatre gave Fox West Coast a strong presence outside of downtown Los Angeles.

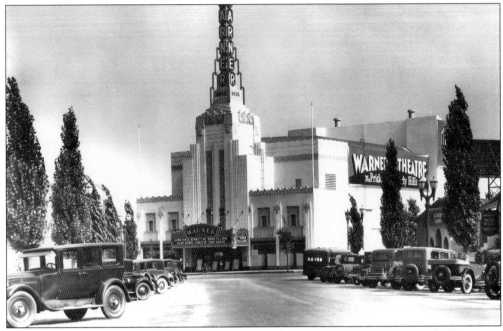

WARNER THEATRE BEVERLY HILLS, 1931. Designed by B. Marcus Priteca, a crew of 150 painters and decorators was employed during the last month of construction to complete the project in time for its debut. The opening was attended by the movie colony in Beverly Hills, including some of the Warner brothers and their families. The theatre was demolished in December 1988 to make room for a parking lot.

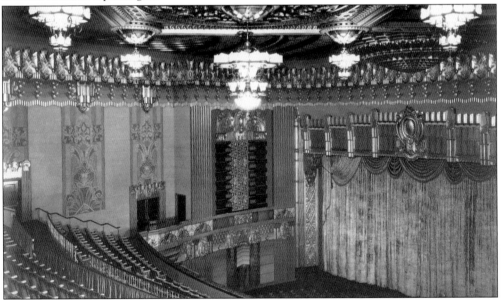

WARNER THEATRE BEVERLY HILLS AUDITORIUM, 1931. The construction of this theatre fulfilled a promise by Beverly Hills resident Jack Warner to build a modern movie palace in his adopted hometown. The interior was Spanish revival, with more than a hint of Art Deco stylization. How fitting that the premiere film in 1931 was *The Millionaire*, starring George Arliss. Even during the Depression, many in the local audience could relate.

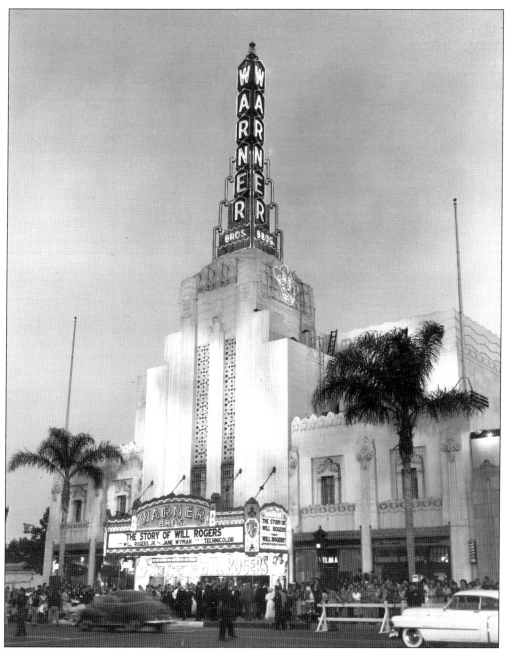

WARNER THEATRE PREMIERE, 1952. Will Rogers once remarked, "The movies are the only business where you can go out front and applaud yourself." The 1952 premiere of *The Story of Will Rogers* was a glamorous yet poignant evening. Will Rogers Jr., played the role of his father in this biopic about one of America's best-loved personalities. Will Sr. seemed to invent the hyphenate as a comedian–actor–satirist–writer–vaudeville performer–movie star. Rogers died in a plane crash near Barrow, Alaska, in 1935. Originally from Oklahoma, Rogers made Beverly Hills his principal residence in the 1920s, and later bought 186 acres in the Pacific Palisades, where he also resided. After his wife's death in 1944, the Will Rogers Ranch became a state park. Will Jr. was elected to Congress in 1942, but resigned in 1944 to join the army as a tank commander.

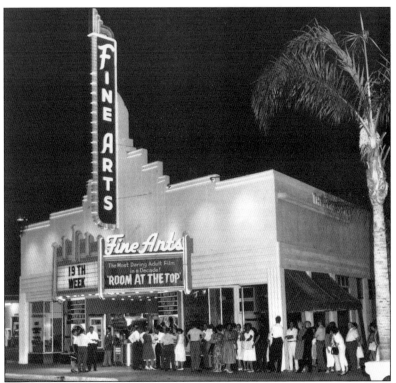

FINE ARTS THEATRE, 1959. When it opened in 1937, this theatre by B. Marcus Priteca and S. E. Sonnichen was called the Wilshire Regina. It was renamed the Fine Arts after a renovation in 1948, just in time to show the ballet film *The Red Shoes*. In 1959, it ran *Room at the Top* for over six months. Still a Deco beauty at 8556 Wilshire Boulevard, it now shows independent films.

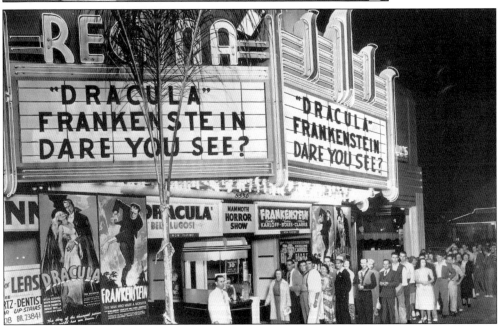

REGINA THEATRE, 1938. Horrors! A midnight show featuring classic monsters aimed to make women clutch their dates in terror. Columnist E. V. Durling thought that the theatre should continue the scream-fest. "All I can suggest . . . is a slow motion picture of a run in a woman's stocking," or a scene where the cook and maid don their hats and quit with guests at the door. Scary? Not even in Beverly Hills.

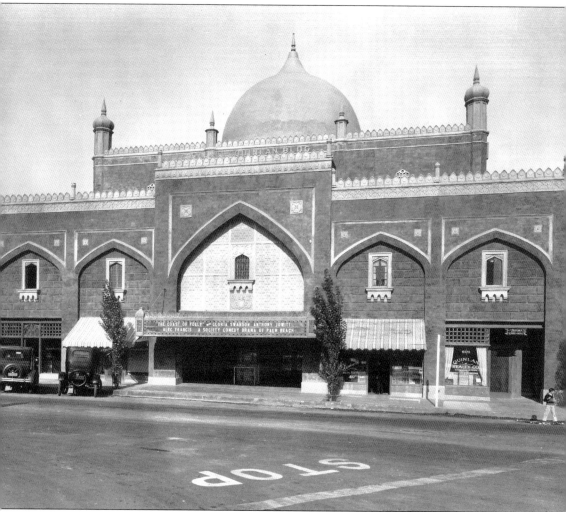

BEVERLY THEATRE, 1925. Designed by L. A. Smith in 1925, the Beverly's East Indian design was a perfect fit for a city brimming with movie moguls. The onion dome and minarets topping the building are characteristic of traditional Indian Mughal architecture—think Taj Mahal. The theatre was built by real estate pioneer Dan M. Quinlan, who maintained offices there and emblazoned his name on top. At the theatre's grand opening, actor Lew Cody proposed to actress Mabel Normand, and they eloped to Ventura several months later, rousting a judge out of bed to marry them at 3:00 a.m. The marriage lasted until her death in 1930. Formerly located at 206 North Beverly Boulevard, just north of Wilshire, the Beverly Theatre was remodeled many times. With each successive renovation more East Indian design features disappeared. It was demolished in 2006 and will be replaced by a luxury hotel.

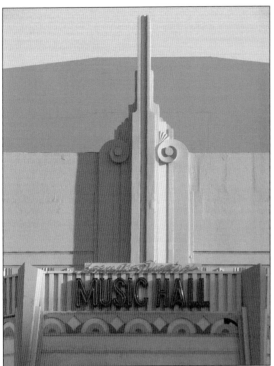

MUSIC HALL. Originally known as the Elite Theatre when it opened in 1936, this building was aptly named for its Beverly Hills location. It was designed by Wilfred B. Verity and is still going strong at 9036 Wilshire Boulevard. Now operated by the Laemmle organization, it was divided into three screens and currently shows art and foreign films. (Frank E. Cooper Jr.)

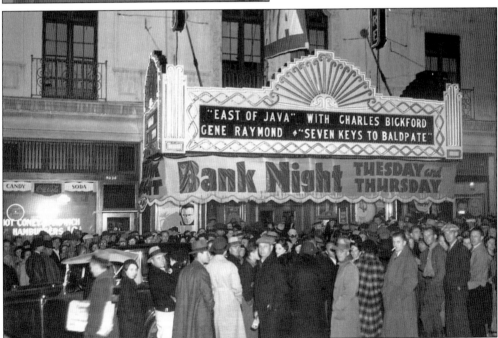

MARQUIS THEATRE, 1936. When the Marquis Theatre at 9038 Melrose Avenue opened on Armistice evening in 1925, it rated barely an inch of newspaper space. Who would have suspected that in 1949, they would be handing out Oscars there? The Academy of Motion Picture Arts and Sciences made the building their headquarters from 1946 to 1975. The Oscars are going strong, but the theatre is no longer there.

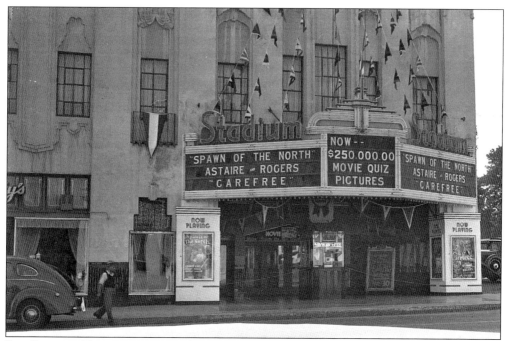

FOX STADIUM THEATRE, 1938. Built as part of the expanding Fox West Coast theatre chain, the Fox Stadium at 8906 West Pico Boulevard is now the Binai David Judea Orthodox Synagogue. Like many Angelenos, architect Carl Boller was a transplanted Midwesterner, migrating from Kansas City in 1921. Carl and his brother Robert designed over 100 theatres primarily in the Midwest and Southwest, including the Kimo in Albuquerque, New Mexico.

LIDO THEATRE, 1945. This multipurpose structure designed in 1937 by Clifford A. Balch at 8507 Pico Boulevard allowed convenient access to a bank and shops before taking in a movie at the 900-seat theatre in the building. During World War II, the Lido contributed to the war effort by selling war bonds. It was used for religious services for many years before it was demolished.

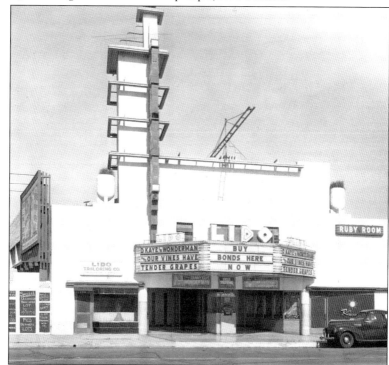

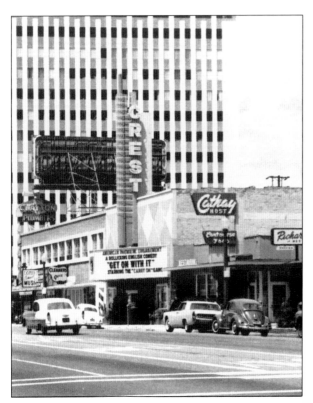

WESTWOOD CREST THEATRE, AKA MAJESTIC CREST, 1963. Built by Frances Seymour Fonda, second wife of Henry Fonda, the Crest Theatre, at 1262 Westwood Boulevard, is a small 500-seat neighborhood theatre in the heart of Westwood. Primarily known for his residential properties in the Westwood area, architect Arthur W. Hawes designed the Crest in 1941.

WESTWOOD CREST DETAIL. Radically remodeled in the 1980s and 1990s, the Crest is trying to maintain its Art Deco history. Now independently owned, the owner is facing the same challenges independent theatre owners in the early 20th century faced: convincing the big movie studios to exhibit their first-run films in his single-screen theatre. (Suzanne Cooper.)

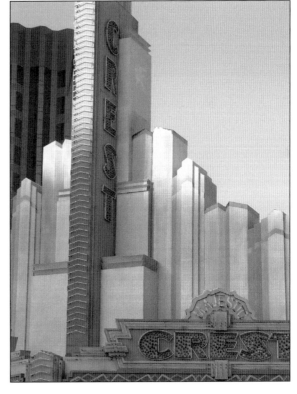

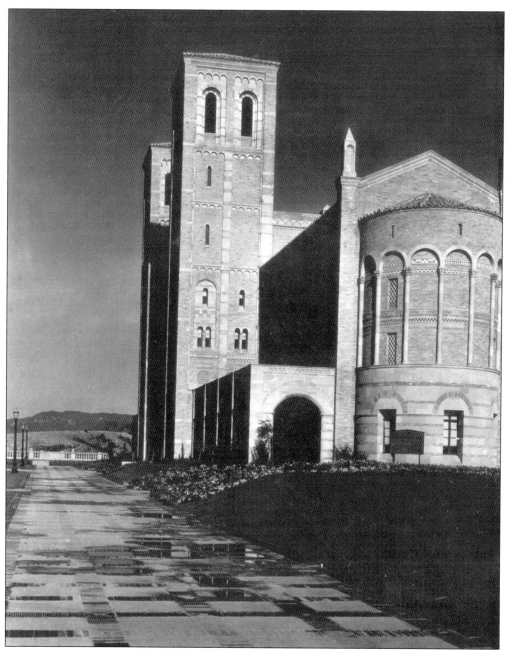

ROYCE HALL. "Thinking is like loving or dying. Each of us must do it for ourselves," opined California-born philosopher Josiah Royce, whose namesake theatre was one of the first buildings constructed at UCLA's new Westwood campus in 1929. It is said that architect Daniel Allison modeled Royce Hall after the Basilica di San Ambrogio, a 12th-century Romanesque church in Italy. Acoustics were important enough to test nine different kinds of plaster with the help of Dr. Vern O. Knudsen, an expert in acoustics who later became chancellor of the university. A special proscenium arch was designed to convey sound to the rear of the auditorium. (Postcard uncredited.)

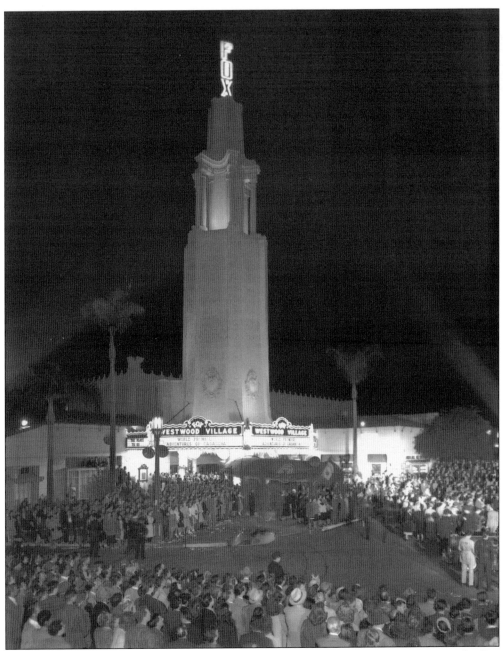

Fox West Coast Village Theatre, 1948. Designed by Percy Parke Lewis in 1931, the Fox West Coast Village Theatre is a Westwood icon famed for its neon-topped tower. Now managed by the Mann theatre chain, the Village Theatre at 961 Broxton Avenue still hosts glamorous movie premieres. The drama in Westwood's first theatre wasn't limited to the silver screen. In January 1932, LAPD lieutenant Hugh Crowley was gunned down in the lobby by two men he caught red-handed in the act of robbing the theatre. The bandits were tried and hanged. This wasn't the detective's first gun battle with theatre bandits. He was involved in a shoot out at Grauman's Chinese Theatre in 1929. Clark Gable was just one of many stars who appeared at a benefit for Crowley's widow.

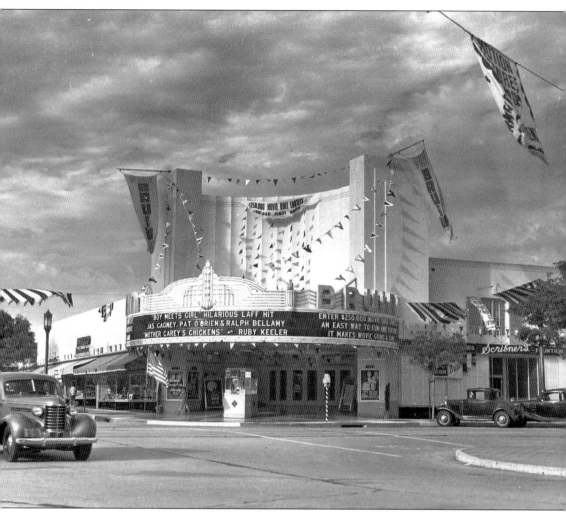

BRUIN THEATRE, 1938. Just across the street from its older sister, the Fox Village, is the Bruin Theatre at 948 Broxton Avenue, designed by S. Charles Lee in 1937. The Moderne concave facade complements the half-circle wraparound marquee that makes it possible to see what's playing from all directions. The marquee was an important aspect of Lee's designs, planned to be eye-catching by day or night. During the daylight hours, one couldn't rely on the flashing spectacle produced by neon, so many of Lee's designs incorporated unique shapes, such as tall towers, circular signage—or a combination of both. Shown here in 1938, the exterior entrance features terrazzo flooring and a freestanding box office. A short walk from UCLA, the Bruin is named after the university's sports teams.

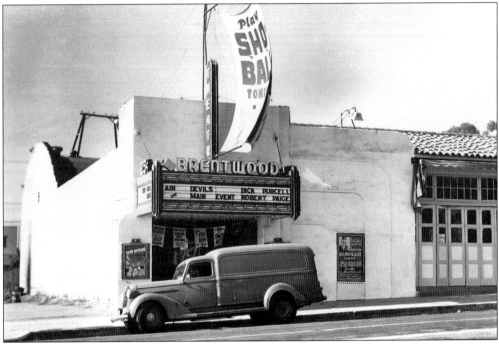

BRENTWOOD THEATRE, 1938. Not much is known about the Brentwood Theatre at 11611 Wilshire Boulevard, possibly designed by Leland Bryant in 1926. Advertisements appeared regularly from 1935 to 1950. It no doubt suffered its share of run-of-the-mill robberies, but one stood out. After enjoying a movie, a couple unlocked their car to leave, only to discover that the steering wheel was missing. The theatre itself is now gone, too.

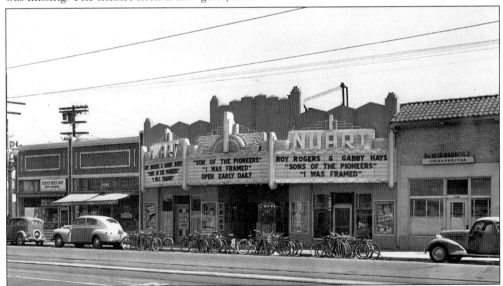

NUART THEATRE, 1942. No doubt the Nuart, at 11272 Santa Monica Boulevard, had a quiet appeal after it opened in the early 1930s. Since the 1970s, however, it has been a popular art house whose schedule once vied with the Fox Venice for space on refrigerators of intellectual film buffs. Not that they take themselves too seriously—*The Rocky Horror Picture Show* still screens at midnight after more than 25 years.

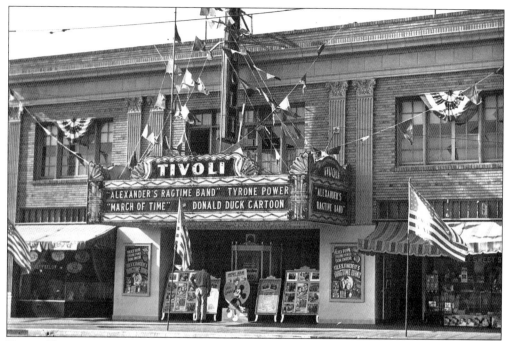

TIVOLI THEATRE, 1938. In the 1920s, the Tivoli Theatre, at 11523 Santa Monica Boulevard, was just another neighborhood movie house, but it made the news in 1932 when the owner and his wife were victims of a daring daylight robbery. Seven months later, the jewels were found with his brother-in-law, and the owner was arrested for insurance fraud. The theatre survives as Laemmle's Royal.

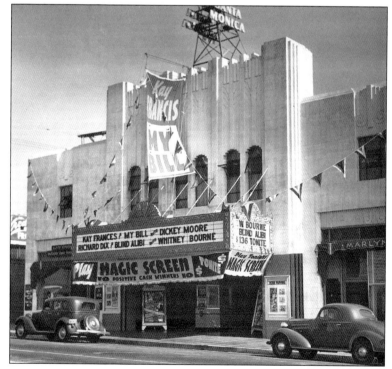

WILSHIRE SANTA MONICA THEATRE, 1938. Now known as the Nu-Wilshire, the theatre is a first-run art house operated by Landmark Theatres. It opened in November 1930 at 1314 Wilshire Boulevard in Santa Monica, then called the "Bay District." Architect John M. Cooper, a Yale graduate and former engineer on the Panama Canal, also designed the Roxie Theatre on South Broadway.

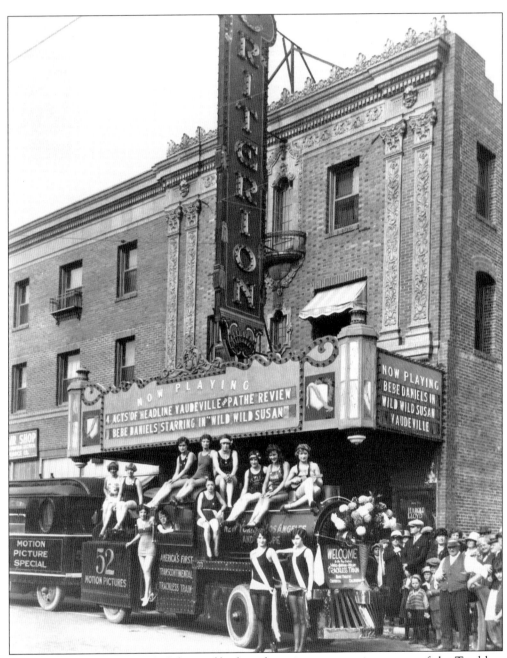

CRITERION THEATRE, 1925. A bevy of bathing beauties came out in support of the Trackless Train when it made a stop at the Criterion Theatre in Santa Monica. The novelty vehicle drove cross-country from New York to Los Angeles, promoting better roads and better motion pictures. Car dealer Harold L. Arnold pointed out, "We have plenty of room for improvement along both lines," but felt that the fact a train weighing 26,000 pounds was able to negotiate the roads "is proof that we have a really good road system now." Sid Grauman was, of course, involved, and journey's end for the Trackless Train was a parking spot in the forecourt of the Egyptian. When the Criterion was built in 1923, it was planned with decorations purported to surpass some famous Los Angeles theatres. The Criterion, at Third Street and Arizona Avenue, is now a six-plex.

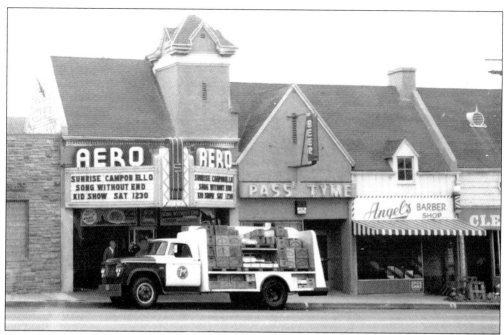

AERO THEATRE, 1960. Built by Donald Douglas of Douglas Aircraft in 1940 as a morale booster for his employees, the Aero was reportedly kept open 24 hours a day in order to accommodate their work schedules. Designed by P. M. Woolpert, it is located at 1328 Montana Avenue in Santa Monica. It is now operated by the American Cinematheque and shows classic and rare films.

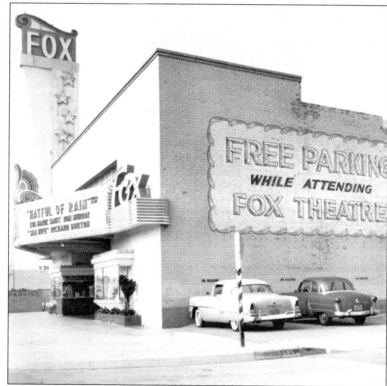

FOX VENICE, 1957. Imagine what a movie could be made: four years after a theatre's star-studded 1951 opening, a storm flooded the lobby. Children attending a Disney matinee had to be rescued by rowboat. Sounds like something the Fox Venice, 620 Lincoln Boulevard, might have screened when it was the hippest art house in the city, famed for classic cinema, cult classics, and live performances before it was a swap meet.

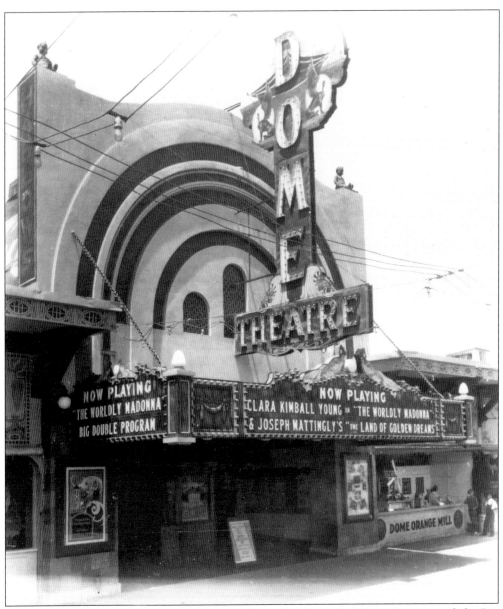

FOX DOME THEATRE, 1922. "Millions for Joy; Not One Cent for Gloom," trumpeted the *Los Angeles Times* in 1922, heralding the building of the Ocean Park Pier. Less than two years later, flames destroyed the amusement area, including two theatres, the Dome and the Rosemary. Plans for replacement began almost immediately and construction started on the new, improved Dome Theatre. The architecture was variously described as Spanish, Egyptian, and Moorish, with design attributed to Engineering Service of Los Angeles, although mention has also been made of Clifford A. Balch. The original headline could have been dusted off in 1929, followed by a familiar theme song beginning "M-I-C-K-E-Y," when the Fox Dome Theatre formed the very first Mickey Mouse Club. Precursors to the television show, these real clubs showed cartoons, recited credos, and elected a Chief Mickey and Chief Minnie Mouse. Unfortunately nothing is eternal except maybe Mickey Mouse. Done in by decay and a series of fires in the 1970s, Ocean Park Pier, by then called "P.O.P.," was destroyed, taking everything but memories with it.

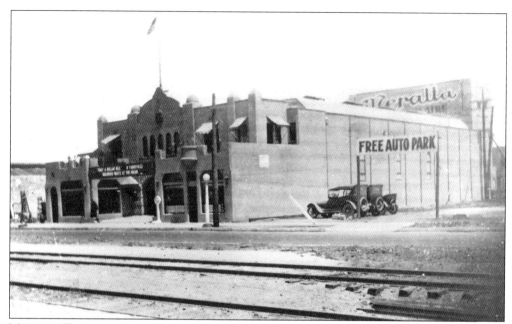

MERALTA THEATRE, 1924. The large Pearl Merrill and tiny Laura Peralta performed in vaudeville as "Ella Fant and Miss Kito" but soon tired of traveling and built a theatre. They moved to 9632 Culver Boulevard in 1924. Opening fanfare included Will Rogers, Thomas Ince's new film, and an Our Gang comedy where all the kids leaped through their on-screen likenesses when the projectionist stopped the film.

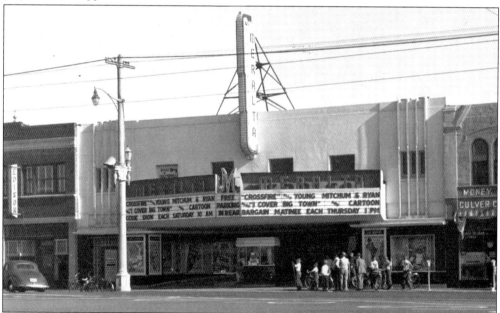

MERALTA THEATRE, 1947. In 1943, eight years after a C. A. Balch remodel, fire swept through the theatre. With a World War II building moratorium in effect, the Meralta relocated for several years before rebuilding. After Pearl Merrill's death in 1961, Laura Peralta Brackett remained in her apartment over the theatre, constructed so she could watch the films from a special room. In 1983, an office building replaced the theatre.

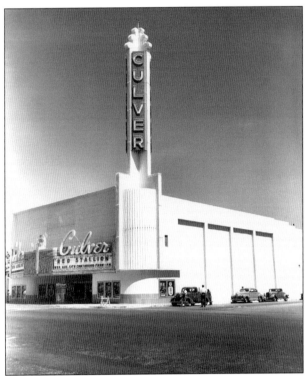

CULVER THEATRE, 1947. Despite its location in the shadow of the historic MGM studio lot, the Culver Theatre at 9820 Washington Boulevard no longer shows films. The theatre originally opened in 1945, and the interior was completely gutted and modernized in 2004 when it became a live theatre named for Kirk Douglas. The box office and terrazzo sidewalk have been restored, but the original script neon sign was removed and put in storage.

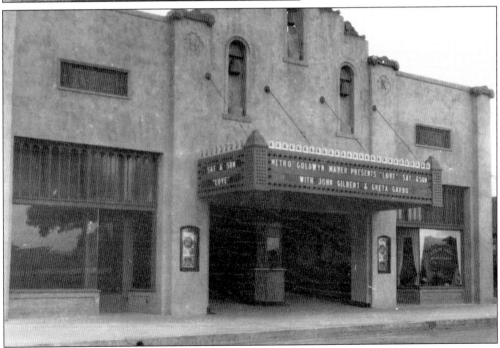

PALMS THEATRE, 1928. It's rarely possible to trace a small, neighborhood theatre as it changes with the years. This photograph shows the Palms Theatre as a simple Spanish-style building. Orlopp and Orlopp designed the theatre in 1926 for owner Henry Kidson, whose initials flank niches holding mission bells. The square-edged marquee was added a year later.

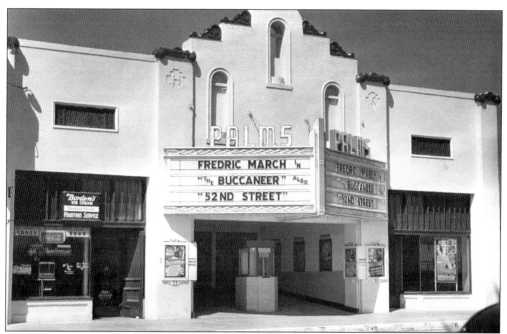

PALMS THEATRE, 1938. The next change to the theatre at 3751 Motor Avenue occurred in the 1930s. The marquee changed shape and neon was added. The niches remained, but the bells were removed, creating a slightly sleeker look. Fredric March starred in Cecil B. DeMille's *The Buccaneer.*

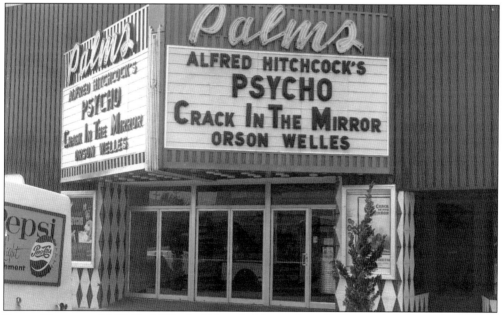

PALMS THEATRE, 1960. By 1985, the Palms, hidden under a 1960s metal shell, symbolized the clash between the beloved old and the necessary new: a cozy neighborhood theatre demolished for a bigger post office. The theatre had other tales to tell: a missing four-year-old found, the ability to host a festival's older films when newer theatres couldn't handle flammable nitrate film, and, as always, everyday stories of movies seen and loved.

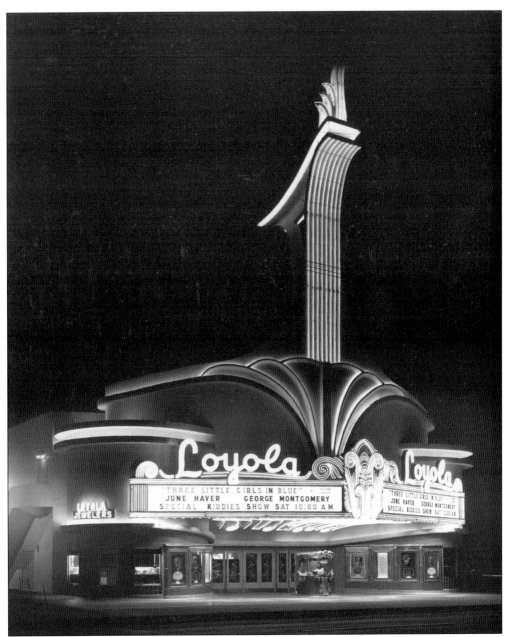

LOYOLA THEATRE, 1946. Designed as a first-run theatre for Charles P. Skouras, president of Fox West Coast, Clarence Smale's exuberant and swanlike Loyola Theatre at 8610 South Sepulveda Boulevard is a late-Deco masterpiece. Proceeds from the 1946 opening were donated to its nearby namesake school, Loyola University, earmarked for dormitories and academic facilities to serve returning World War II veterans. When the theatre closed in 1982, Mickey Cottrell, its last manager, gave it a poetic eulogy: "Theatres like the Loyola are the cathedrals of America, our heritage, where we went to dream a little." He added that another part of our heritage is greed, "and I'm afraid it is destroying our landmarks." The city couldn't keep the Westchester theatre open but did designate it an historic monument, preventing the developer from destroying the facade. The graceful pylon, elaborate box office, and terrazzo entrance are still there to be admired.

Five

North

STUDIO CITY THEATRE,
1938. How better to announce
a theatre than with the
multicolored glow of neon? It
sounds so simple: a glass tube
filled with neon, argon, or
another gas, bent to the desired
shape, but spark that tube with
electricity, and the result is pure
magic. Los Angeles was once
home to a treasure trove of neon
signs, beckoning customers
not only to theatres, but also
to restaurants, stores, hotels
and apartment buildings. The
Studio City Theatre at 12136
Ventura Boulevard opened
in 1938 with a fine display of
light, but it took more than
gorgeous neon to impress their
larger neighbor to the south.
The *Los Angeles Times* gave
the theatre barely a mention,
informing their readers that
the Gore brothers and Adolph
Ramish were "associated with"
the theatre, under a headline
speculating that Ed Wynn
would play the Wizard of Oz.
Only the building permit
seemed to care that Clifford A.
Balch was the architect.

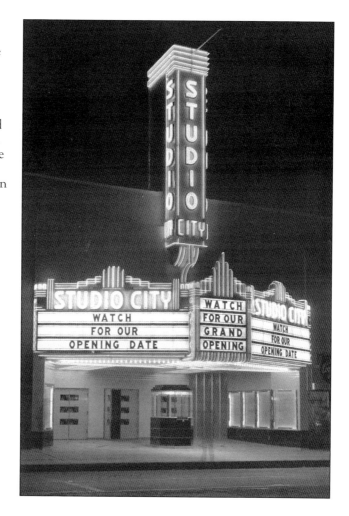

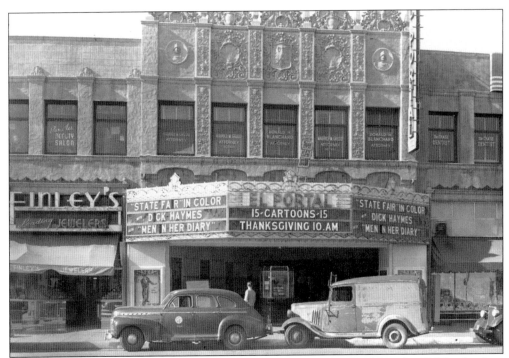

EL PORTAL THEATRE, 1945. Beautifully restored as a working theatre, the El Portal at 5267 Lankershim Boulevard in North Hollywood dates its history to 1926. Its official Web site describes it as having "weathered the Jazz Age, the Depression, 4 wars, and finally the great earthquake of 1994." Designed by L. A. Smith, the theatre's life span has included silents, talkies, and live theatre.

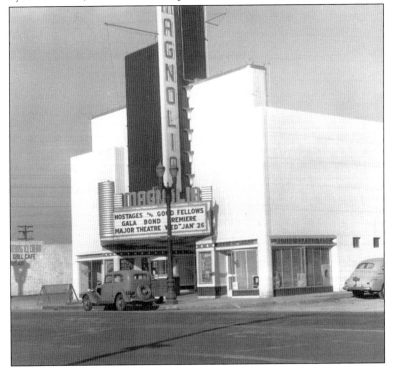

MAGNOLIA THEATRE, 1944. Architect Jacques de Forest Griffin envisioned a theatre in 1929, built in a modified French style and topped by a 170-foot pylon inspired by the Eiffel Tower. Burbank city councilman Bob Bowne complained in 1985 that it was an embarrassment that the city had no walk-in theatres. Too bad they didn't keep this Art Deco gem at Magnolia Boulevard and Hollywood Way open.

LA REINA THEATRE, 1938. With its name reflecting Southern California's Hispanic heritage, the La Reina at 14626 Ventura Boulevard in Sherman Oaks was not treated in a very queenly manner in 1987 when it was threatened with demolition. Its interior was gutted in the 1980s, and it now houses shops. The facade, box office, and terrazzo remain.

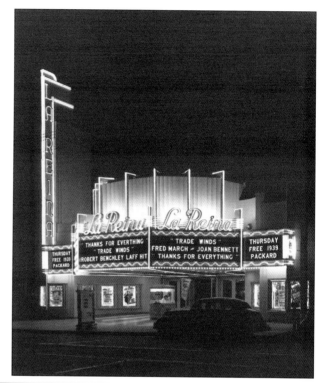

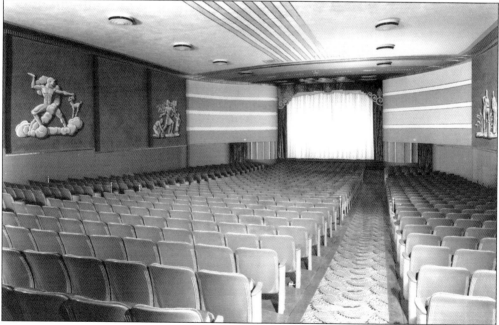

LA REINA THEATRE AUDITORIUM, 1938. Designed by S. Charles Lee, this former neighborhood theatre was built in 1938. Lee simplified the auditorium design, replacing ornate embellishments with pared down artwork. This had two important benefits: Simpler designs contributed to better acoustics, and it was a far more economical way to build a theatre during the Depression years when Lee was among the architects who popularized the Streamline Moderne style.

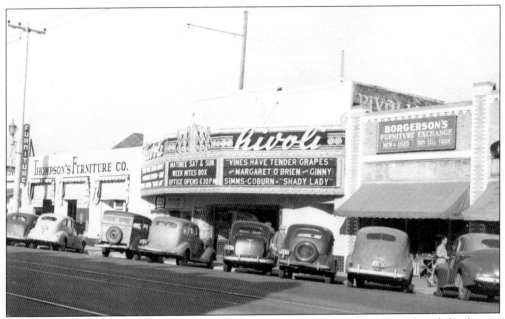

RIVOLI THEATRE, 1945. From 1913, when Van Nuys's very first factory opened, until the demise of silent film, the town was famous for pipe organs, so it was news when the hometown Rivoli Theatre installed one. Very little else about the theatre was considered newsworthy. When the *Los Angeles Times* announced the new playhouse in 1924, they merely said that it was "generally believed to be a West Coast Theatre."

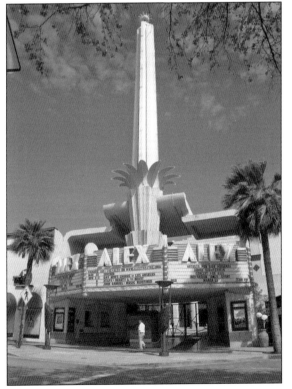

ALEX THEATRE. The Alexander at 216 North Brand Boulevard in Glendale opened in 1925 for movies and vaudeville. The original design by Charles R. Selkirk and Arthur G. Lindley had a long forecourt and small marquee, barely noticeable even to the most alert passerby. In 1939, S. Charles Lee added the 100-foot-tall neon tower topped with a starburst and three-sided marquee that still beckons patrons to the beautifully restored theatre. (Frank E. Cooper Jr.)

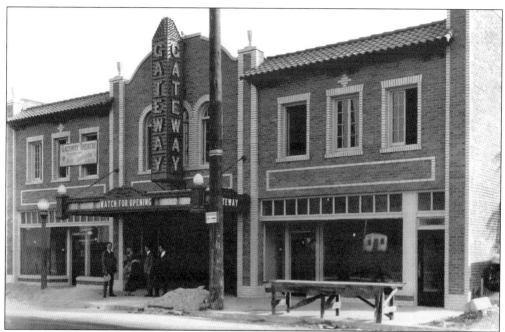

GATEWAY THEATRE, 1923. Just after the advent of talking pictures, the Gateway Theater at 3731 San Fernando Road in Glendale tried an unusual experiment after hard-of-hearing patrons complained that they couldn't understand the actors. A microphone was positioned directly in front of the speakers to broadcast dialogue to individual headsets. The theatre, one of many built c. 1923 and decorated in the Egyptian style, did not last as long as Tutankhamen's tomb.

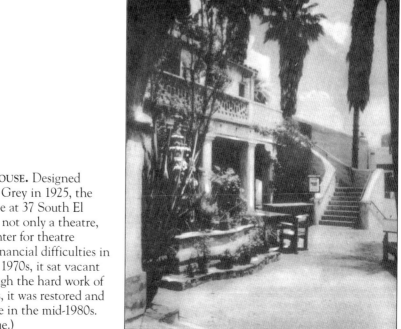

PASADENA PLAYHOUSE. Designed by architect Elmer Grey in 1925, the Pasadena Playhouse at 37 South El Molino Avenue, is not only a theatre, but also a local center for theatre education. After financial difficulties in the late 1960s and 1970s, it sat vacant for 16 years. Through the hard work of alumni and friends, it was restored and brought back to life in the mid-1980s. (Postcard by Artvue.)

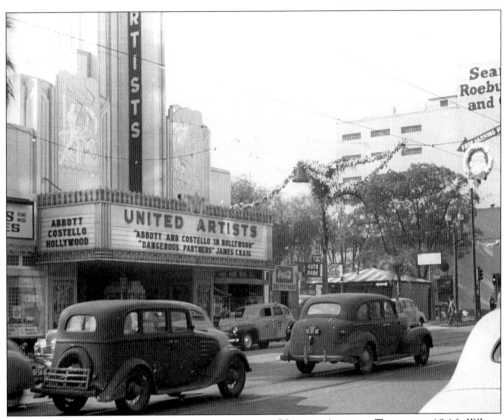

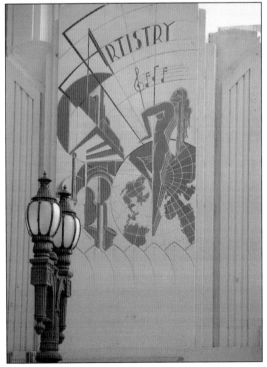

UNITED ARTISTS THEATRE, 1946. When Walker and Eisen and Clifford Balch were hired by United Artists in 1931 to give their theatres a recognizable look, the theatre at 606 East Colorado Boulevard in Pasadena featured prominently in drawings distributed to the press. The building now sells school supplies: kids might prefer a matinee, but teachers appreciate the tools available to train budding artists to read, write, and paint.

UNITED ARTISTS THEATRE ARTISTRY PANEL. Because United Artists was founded by some of the most prominent names in the film industry, it seems appropriate that their theatres would feature both *Unity* and *Artistry*. This marvelously Deco panel, and its mate, *Unity*, were uncovered when a 1960s facade was removed during the building's conversion to retail space. (Suzanne Cooper.)

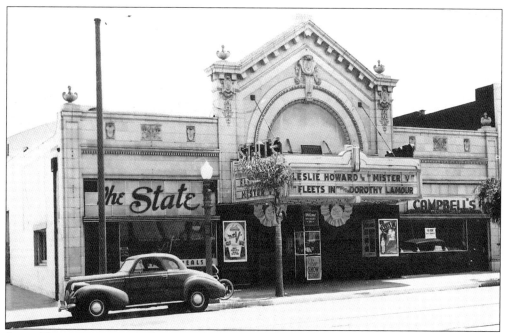

STATE THEATRE, 1942. Much was made of the fact that Oliver P. Dennis was a Pasadena architect when he designed the Florence Theatre in 1917. By the 1940s, the theatre at 770 East Colorado Boulevard was the State. Part of its sign was rescued by the Museum of Neon Art, which celebrates and preserves Southern California's neon heritage.

ACADEMY THEATRE, 1946. When the Academy Theatre at 1003 East Colorado Boulevard opened in 1924 as Bard's Pasadena, the interior was said to be adapted from the ballroom of Ramses II. No word on whether their prize-winning Rose Parade float in 1926 depicted the pharaoh fox-trotting or dancing the Charleston. L. A. Smith's original architecture was modernized in 1958 by Carl Moeller, and later was made into an uninspiring six-plex.

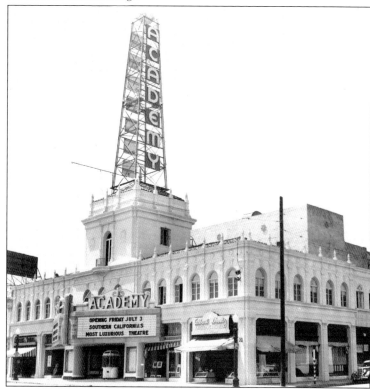

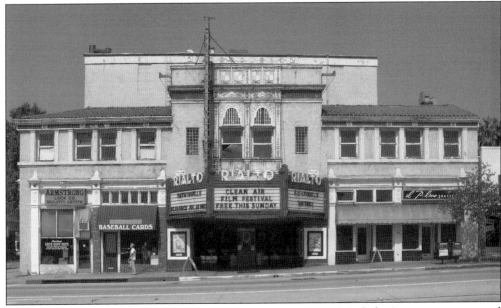

RIALTO THEATRE. Opened in 1925, the Rialto Theatre at 1023 Fair Oaks Avenue was supposed to be a success story, but "progress" can outdate a book even before publication. L A. Smith's 1925 building survived 82 years and two fires, but the theatre, with its Batchelder tile drinking fountain, harpies, and red-eyed gargoyle glaring down closed in August 2007. South Pasadena citizens saved it from developers in 1977. Will history repeat itself? (Frank E. Cooper Jr.)

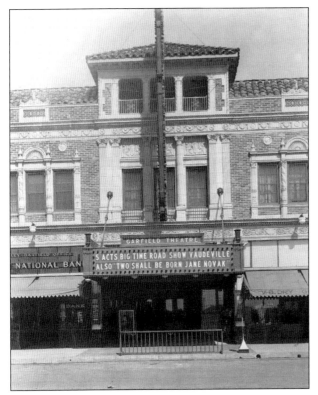

GARFIELD THEATRE, 1925. A thousand people were turned away from the opening of the Garfield Egyptian Theatre in 1924, when Alhambra was a thinly settled town amidst waving grain. By 1985, the population had changed. The Garfield sold shrimp chips and soybean drinks to customers lining up for the latest action flick from Taiwan. Alhambra is no longer sparsely populated, and the theatre, attributed to L. A. Smith, is not in business.

Six

SOUTH

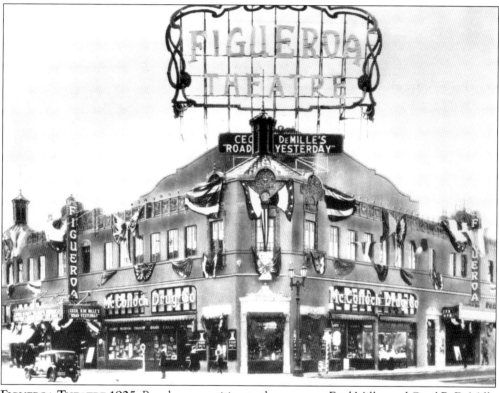

FIGUEROA THEATRE 1925. Popular superstition to the contrary, Fred Miller and Cecil B. DeMille agreed that Friday the 13th, 1925, was an opening date that could only bring good fortune . . . or at least good press. They must have been right. An opening night critic wrote, "The gods have favored Cecil B. DeMille in the choice of show house for the world premiere showing of his great new spectacular production, *The Road to Yesterday*. It has been placed in Fred Miller's new $1,000,000 Figueroa Theatre." W. S. Hebbard's design was described as medieval Spanish, with the colors of Castile and Aragon mingled with those of the Aztecs. A frieze of fruits of California—oranges, lemons, and pomegranates—was outlined in tile. The furnishings were imported from Spain, including a 200-year-old table that was the centerpiece of the lobby. But Lady Luck is fickle. In 1968, her gaze fell on the theatre near Exposition Park, and 508 West Santa Barbara Avenue (now Martin Luther King Boulevard) became a gas station.

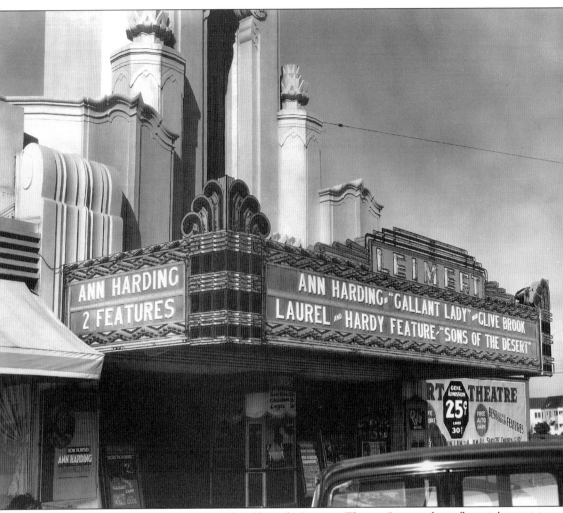

LEIMERT THEATRE, 1933. "Artists should see the Leimert Theatre," wrote the influential art critic Arthur Millier in 1932, a year after the theatre at 3341 West Forty-third Place opened. He was impressed by the architecture of Morgan, Walls and Clements, and described the oval auditorium with its widely spaced rows as "free from rubbishy ornament." His highest praise went to Andre Durenceau's mural *Sampson and Delilah*, which he compared favorably to Rubens. In 1968, the building was purchased by Jehovah's Witnesses and later was sold to actress Marla Gibbs, who created a performing arts center known as the Vision Theatre. Her dream came to an end in 1997, when she couldn't raise enough cash to keep it afloat, a great disappointment to the strong African American cultural movement in Leimert Park. The theatre was taken over by the City of Los Angeles and is currently in use through the Department of Cultural Affairs.

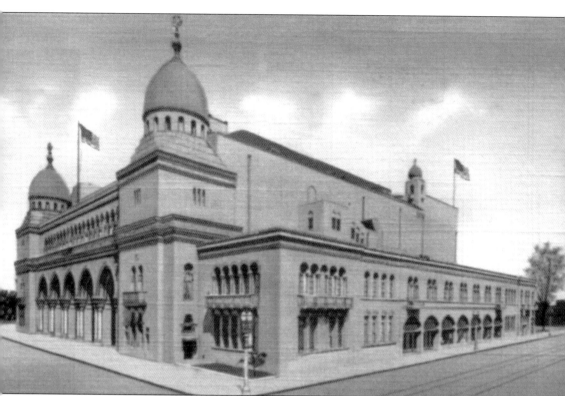

SHRINE AUDITORIUM. The original Los Angeles home of the Shriners was built in 1906. It dramatically burned down in 1920 and was rebuilt by the membership of the Al Malaikah, which translates from Arabic as "city of angels." It is a chapter of the Shrine of North America, aka "the Shriners," a Masonic order founded in 1872 known for philanthropic work, especially hospitals and medical care for children. The new Shrine Auditorium opened at 665 West Jefferson Boulevard to great fanfare in February 1926. Designed by architects John C. Austin, A. M. Edelman, and G. Albert Lansburgh, the building was declared a National Historic Monument in 1975. Besides its neo-Moorish style, massive seems to be the theme. The auditorium seats 6,500 people, and the stage alone is more than 13,000 square feet. When it opened, it boasted the largest stage switchboard in the world, measuring 26 feet long and 9 feet high, with a capacity of over 1,000 watts. In the late 1980s, 1990s, and 2000s, the Shrine hosted the Academy, Grammy, and Emmy Awards. (Courtesy of Rory Cunningham.)

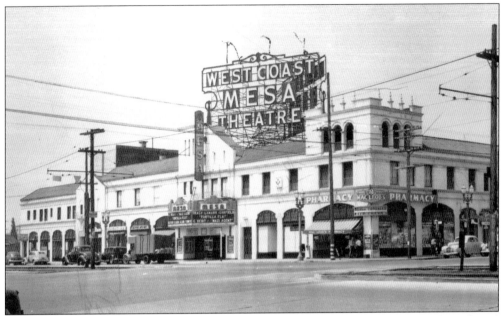

MESA THEATRE, 1942. The Mesa Theatre at Mesa (now part of Crenshaw Boulevard) and Slauson Avenue opened to minor fanfare in 1926 with stars and a film that are unmemorable today. It was one of many in the West Coast Theater chain designed by L. A. Smith. In 1948, it served a grimmer purpose as the primary selective service location in southwest Los Angeles, where young men could register for the draft.

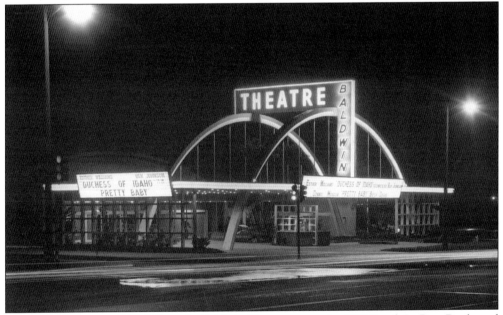

BALDWIN THEATRE, 1950. When the Baldwin Theatre opened at 3741 South La Brea Boulevard in 1949, the construction was widely lauded as innovative. Lewis E. Wilson designed the structure, said to be the first theatre supported entirely by laminated wood arches. Decades later, the remnants, sans the spanning arches that spilled multicolored neon over the facade, bear an uncanny resemblance to a large wasp's nest appended to a mini-mall.

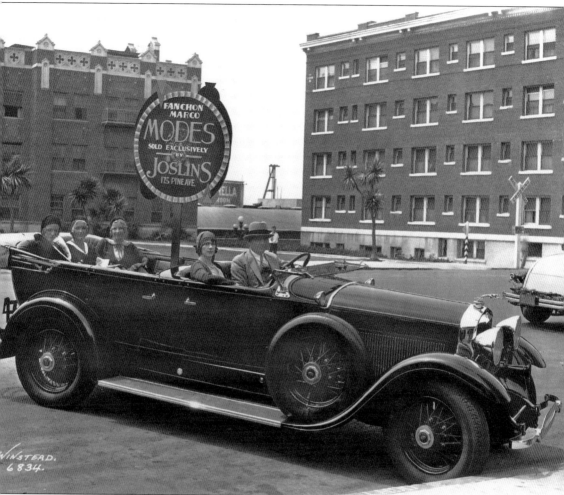

FANCHON AND MARCO. Fanchon and Marco were a brother-and-sister dance act that became phenomenally successful in the 1930s by putting on short musical stage shows before movies. They grew up in the Los Angeles area, where Marco was a newsboy for the *Los Angeles Times*, and the siblings won a scholarship contest that enabled them to study music. In their professional heyday, they directed a ballet school, ran a staff that included set designers and costumers, sent as many as 48 troupes of 24 dancers to locations all over the country, and eventually branched out into managing theatres. As the initial operators of the Baldwin Theatre, their lawsuit to gain access to first-run movies failed. The more prestigious Westwood theatres got premieres; the Baldwin was reduced to "blaxploitation" and previously released films. (Courtesy of the Long Beach Public Library.)

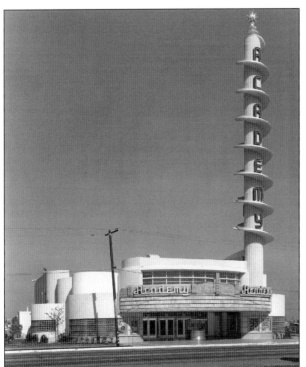

ACADEMY THEATRE, 1939.
There were two sleek and elegant debuts in November 1939 with the premiere of *Another Thin Man* at the Academy Theatre at 3100 West Manchester Boulevard in Inglewood. William Powell and Myrna Loy glided through the innovative S. Charles Lee design for Fox West Coast Theatres. The ultimate in Streamline Moderne design, topped by a striking 125-foot spiral neon tower visible for miles, is now a church.

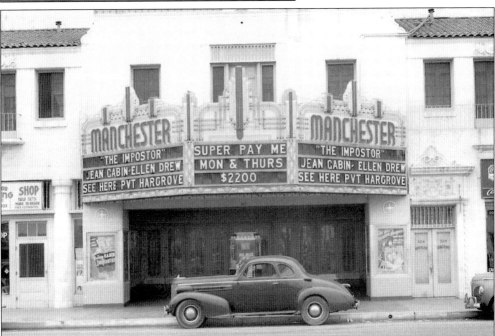

MANCHESTER THEATRE, 1944. *Bluebeard's Seven Wives* played centerpiece at the 1926 gala opening of West Coast's new theatre, attributed to L. A. Smith. Theda Bara and other celebrities were also treated to music and dance acts in the East Indian–style theatre on Manchester Avenue. Fanchon and Marco later used the stage as a testing ground for young dancers. The Wurlitzer Organ was donated to Loyola Marymount University in 1974.

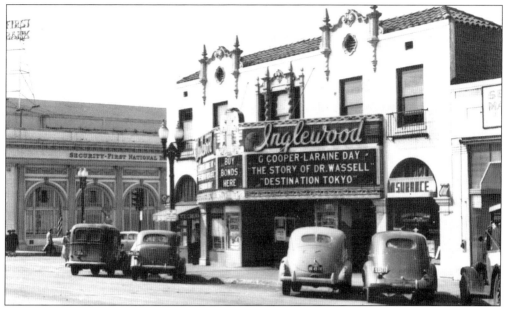

INGLEWOOD THEATRE, 1944. Inglewood's first motion picture house was designed by Carl Boller about 1922. The Spanish-style building was leased to DeWitt B. Van Derlip, who managed a number of theatres. In 1929, he received the most expensive airmail package up to that time, bearing stamps worth $967.60. The postmaster averred that the 625 pounds of advertising brochures cost the government $4,062.00 to fly from Buffalo to the West Coast.

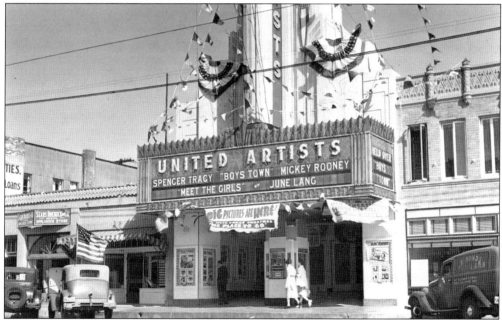

UNITED ARTISTS THEATRE, 1938. In 1931, United Artists announced a plan to standardize their theatres, so patrons would recognize the architecture immediately. Walker and Eisen and C. A. Balch were hired to design approximately 30 theatres in California, including the one at 142 North Market Street in Inglewood. Among the hallmarks of their design were a tall, central pylon and relief panels representing Unity and Artistry.

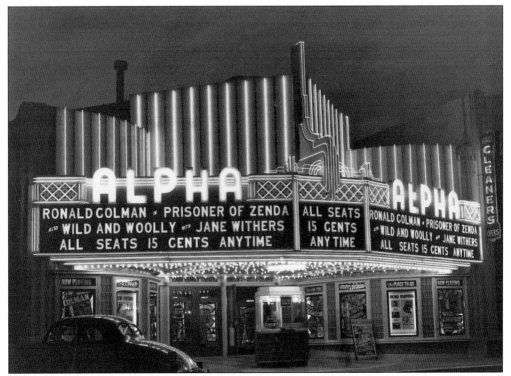

ALPHA THEATRE, 1938. In 1975, when "Saturday morning kiddie matinees could no longer keep a movie house financially solvent," Stan Oftelie wrote a eulogy to the theatres of southeast Los Angeles. By then, he said, the Alpha Theatre (allegedly by S. Charles Lee) was used by the Bell Park and Recreation Department as an all-purpose hall and "the place where cinematic six-guns once blazed . . . offers cake decorating classes."

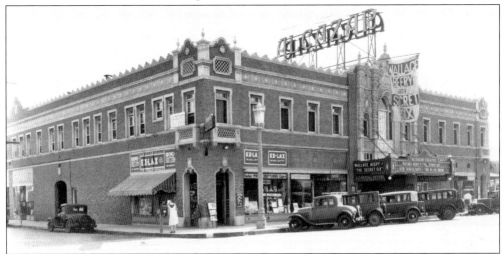

ALCAZAR THEATRE, 1931. Contractor W. M. Bell announced the pending completion of the Alcazar Theatre in March 1925, although the 1,800 seats and pipe organ were yet to be installed at 4426 East Gage Avenue. In 1944, a fire, probably kindled by a forgotten cigarette, caused extensive damage to the interior, although the theatre—attributed to architect J. T. Zeller—served audiences in Bell for many more years.

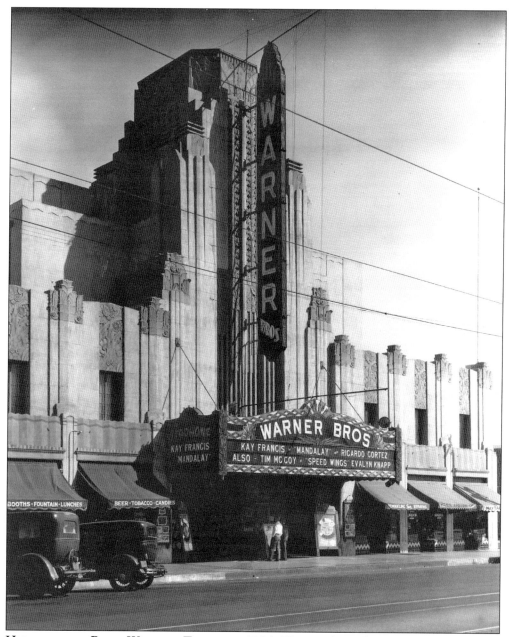

HUNTINGTON PARK WARNER THEATRE, 1934. Two modern theatres were announced simultaneously in 1930. Both, like the Warner Theatre in Beverly Hills, were designed by B. Marcus Priteca as mini-movie palaces with superb Art Nouveau/Deco relief details. Both fell on hard times, but the Warner Huntington Park is now closed with its future unknown, while San Pedro's Warner Grand has been restored to its original elegance.

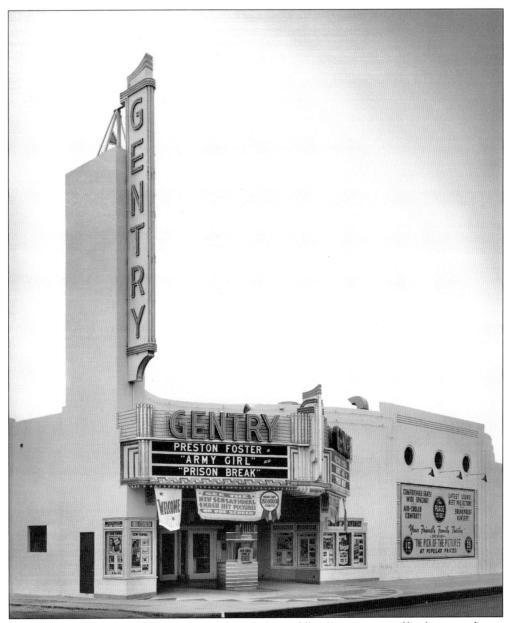

GENTRY THEATRE, 1938. "For 50 cents we took the middle-class man out of his home and gave him an environment that only the church had given before," the most prolific architect of Art Deco theatres in Los Angeles once stated. One hates to contradict S. Charles Lee, but his 1937 Gentry Theatre had impeccable Streamline Moderne styling that has never been seen gracing any church. Speedlines streaked over portholes, evoking a sleek, new ocean liner. A neon-wrapped pylon thrust skyward, and a rounded stairstep pattern echoed the ziggurats popular in the previous decade. An earlier theatre on the site had a run of bad luck. The Sunbeam Theatre at 6525 Compton Avenue was first destroyed when film exploded in the projection room in 1923. The facade crumbled again in 1931 after a mysterious blast, which police speculated was the work of either burglars or union sympathizers. S. Charles Lee's design has fared a bit better. The pylon tenuously remains over dilapidated retail space.

Seven

BEACH CITIES

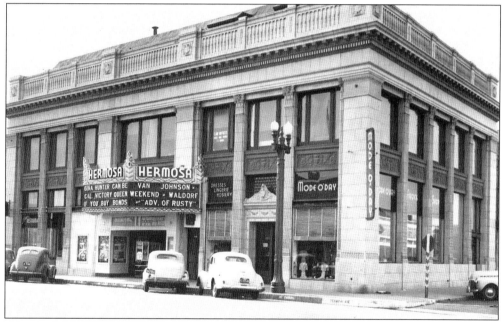

HERMOSA THEATRE, 1945. In 1921, Hermosa Beach was described by W. A. Snyder, the secretary of the local chamber of commerce, as two miles of clean, white sand with no kewpie dolls or hot dog stands. Two years later, a new theatre was announced. Richard D. King was the architect and the name was chosen in a contest. "The Metropolitan" won the $10 gold piece, but by the time it converted to sound in 1929, the theatre was called the Hermosa, and obviously remained that way at least until this picture was taken in 1945. It later became the Bijou, and is now an art gallery at 1225 Hermosa Avenue. The most amazing part of Snyder's claims? In 1921, before the 405 Freeway, where rush hour is all day long, he averred it was possible to travel from Hermosa Beach to Los Angeles in a mere half hour, a feat that can only be equaled today at approximately 2:00 a.m.

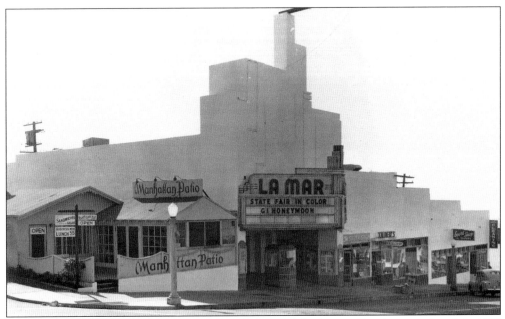

LA MAR THEATRE, 1945. The first movie theatre in Manhattan Beach opened in July 1938 at what was then Central (now Manhattan Beach Boulevard and Highland Avenue). The Art Deco building, designed by Clifford A. Balch for Pacific State Theatres, featured sea motifs, as befitted its beach city location. The theatre closed in the late 1970s.

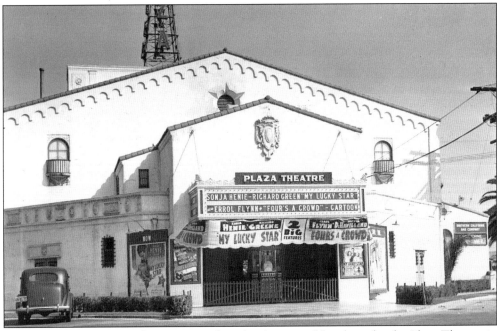

PLAZA THEATRE, 1938. Plans were in place for the ground breaking for the Plaza Theatre in Hawthorne, designed by J. J. Frankenfelder in 1926. Four years later, it was announced that the theatre would gain the unique distinction of being one of the first to be surrounded by a miniature golf course, known as the Fox Movietone News Course. It had 18 holes arranged to evoke a trip around the world.

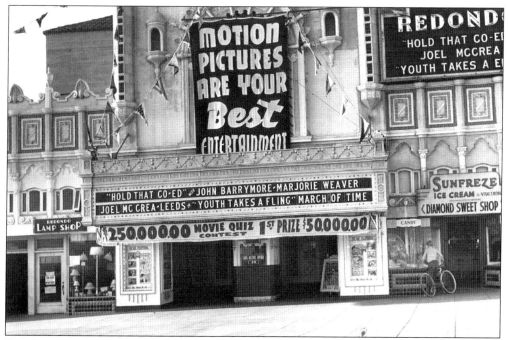

FOX REDONDO, 1938. Designed by John Paxton Perrine, the Fox Redondo was erected on Diamond Avenue in 1928. Idyllic murals showed people gazing down at movie patrons glancing upwards. By 1973, when the cavernous theatre was torn down, teenage boys scared their dates with tales of wharf rats invading the theatre from the nearby Redondo Beach Pier. Wonder if *Hold that Coed* in 1938 elicited more gentlemanly behavior.

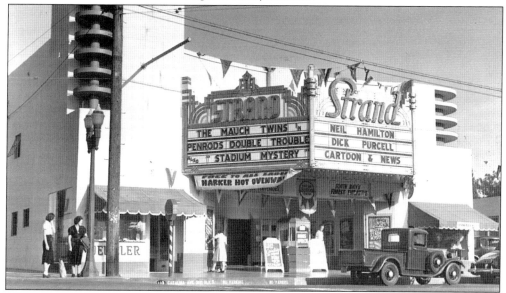

STRAND THEATRE, 1938. The Pacific State Theatre chain's 1937 plans called for their new theatre at Catalina Avenue and Torrance Boulevard to be furnished in the same modern manner as their recently opened El Rey. Originally the Strand, the theatre was later the site of 1970s movie dates for Redondo Beach residents when it was a triplex called the Marina, but eventually it was torn down.

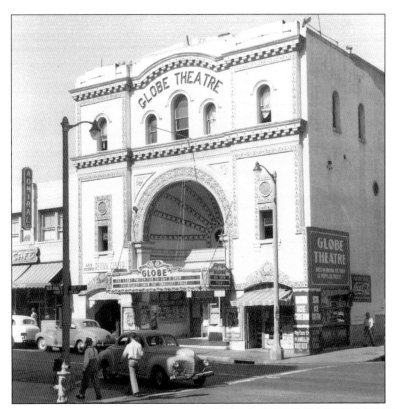

GLOBE THEATRE, 1943. In 1912, the Globe Amusement Company announced plans for its fifth theatre. The Italian marble and stucco structure at Palos Verdes and Sixth Streets in San Pedro, like other Globe theatres, featured a revolving searchlight atop a dome. A newsreel theatre in 1930, it was seriously damaged in the 1933 Long Beach earthquake. No traces remain.

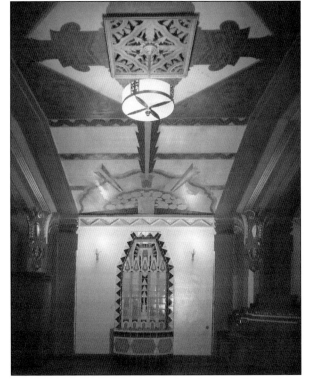

WARNER GRAND. Jack Warner labeled it "the castle of your dreams," when the Warner Grand, designed by B. Marcus Priteca with interiors by A. T. Heinsbergen, opened in San Pedro in 1931. The theatre at 478 West Sixth Street survived unscathed to show newsreel footage of the 1933 Long Beach earthquake, but time took its toll, until another dream came true: The Art Deco masterpiece is being lovingly restored. (Frank E. Cooper Jr.)

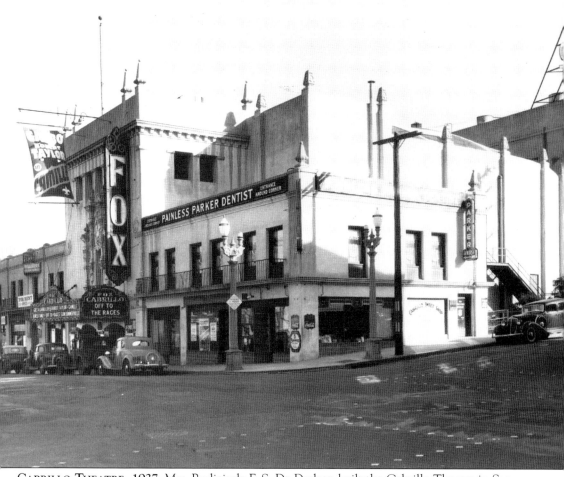

CABRILLO THEATRE, 1937. Mrs. Rudicinda F. S. De Dodson built the Cabrillo Theatre in San Pedro to commemorate her grandfather, Don Jose De Sepulveda, from whom she inherited a good portion of the Palos Verdes Peninsula. De Sepulveda received a grant from the King of Spain, entitling him to land from Point Fermin to Redondo. The theatre, designed by Meyer and Holler and named for explorer Juan Rodriguez Cabrillo, opened with a five-act vaudeville performance and a Western titled *The Bad Man* in 1923. Every one of the 1,600 seats sold out, filled with patrons eagerly gazing at the Spanish galleon on the curtain and waiting for the lights to go out and the show to begin. Years later, the theatre was leveled so people could wait, impatient and annoyed, for someone to give them a parking space.

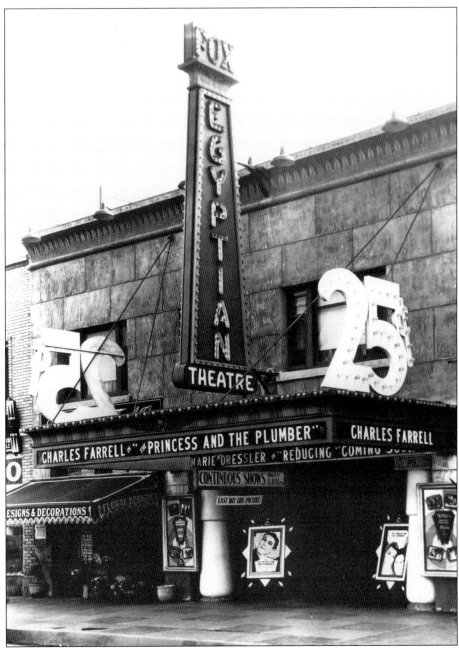

EGYPTIAN THEATRE, 1930. People have been fascinated by ancient Egypt since the time of the pyramids, but what could be better than the Temple of Isis filtered through S. Charles Lee? Perhaps it's what the pharaoh would have wanted had electricity existed in ages B.C. Of course, in 1923, when the theatre on East Fourth Street was designed for A. F. Cheroske, Isis, the Egyptian goddess, would have appeared on film as a movie vamp like Theda Bara. In a story melodramatic enough to have come from a silent film, the theatre's first manager put a bullet in his brain during a drunken, jealous frenzy, while the pretty ticket seller he had kidnapped knelt in prayer. Future archaeologists sifting the sands of Long Beach will find no trace of Lee's Egyptian Theatre, but exploring the archives of local newspapers can unearth its tantalizing history.

FOX WEST COAST THEATRE, 1945. Located before its demise at 333 East Ocean Boulevard, the Fox West Coast Theatre, a 1923 design by Meyer and Holler, survived the Long Beach earthquake intact. An eyewitness said, "People started swarming out of the West Coast Theater there. The first of them were just in time to get caught under an avalanche of bricks and mortar falling from a building beside the theatre."

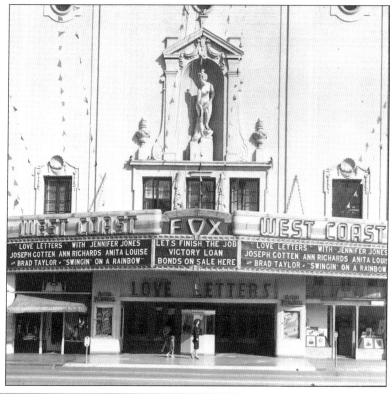

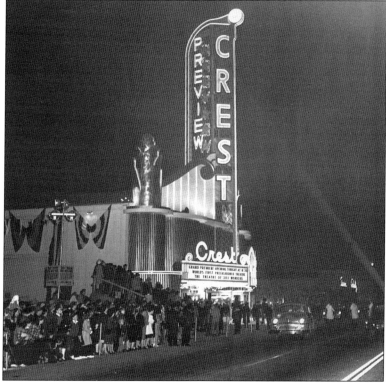

CREST THEATRE 1947. The Crest was a prefabricated theatre that debuted in 1947, "the first of many," according to Fox West Coast president Charles P. Skouras, erected at Atlantic Avenue and Burlingame Drive in Long Beach. Skouras said that the theatre, "which seats 1,164 persons, will be made in Southern California and shipped to wherever films are shown."

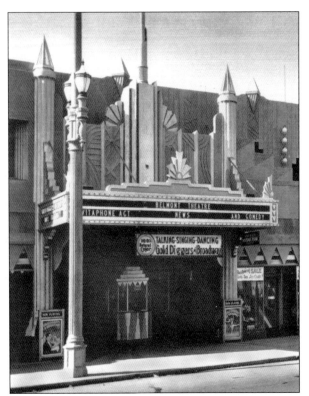

FOX BELMONT. Spectacular in 1929, Reginald F. Inwood's design for 4918 East Second Street could only be described as Deco-meets-Mayan. The interior even had murals of jungle animals. The Long Beach theatre became a gym in the late 1970s, when the sweat required for beauty today supplanted the glamour of the silver screen. Fragments of original design remain on outside walls. (Courtesy of Stan Poe.)

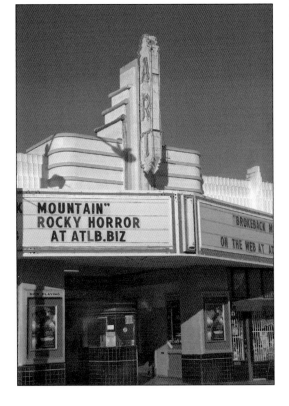

ART THEATRE. The Art Theatre, at 2025 East Fourth Street, is the last remaining neighborhood theatre in Long Beach still showing movies. Spanish style in 1924, a post-quake remodeling by Schilling and Schilling created such Deco flourishes as stepped piers, vertical fluting, a fernlike central pylon, black tile, and a colorful terrazzo floor. A 1947 renovation by Hugh Gibbs added a glass-block wall and remodeled the marquee. (J. Christopher Launi.)

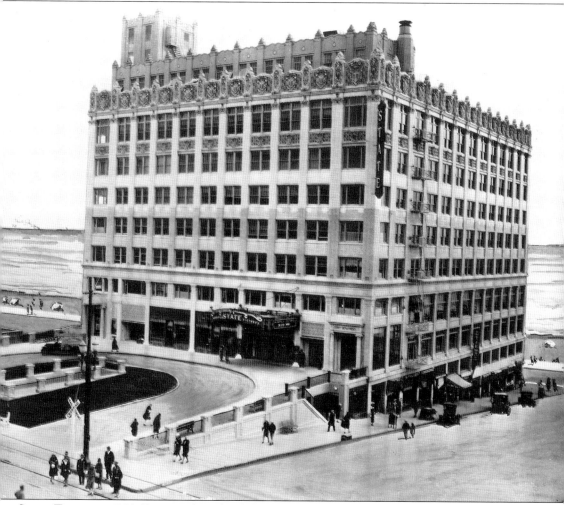

STATE THEATRE, 1929. Despite a fierce battle by preservationists, the Harvey Lockridge–designed Jergins Trust Building at Ocean Boulevard and Pine Avenue was demolished in 1985 to make way for a luxury hotel that was never built. A. T. Jergins was a prominent figure in the oil industry in Long Beach with wells that added $2 million to the city coffers by August 1924. His penthouse office had walnut paneling with a hidden door concealing secret storage space that he probably enjoyed immensely during Prohibition. The building also housed the State Theatre. In 1924, people flocked to the theatre to see *Her Temporary Husband*—not surprising, since the film had been shot in Long Beach and most of the city's then-small population volunteered as extras. An elegant tunnel lined with Italian ceramic tile allowed pedestrians to traverse the distance from the Jergins Trust building to the beach.

DISCOVER THOUSANDS OF LOCAL HISTORY BOOKS
FEATURING MILLIONS OF VINTAGE IMAGES

Arcadia Publishing, the leading local history publisher in the United States, is committed to making history accessible and meaningful through publishing books that celebrate and preserve the heritage of America's people and places.

Find more books like this at
www.arcadiapublishing.com

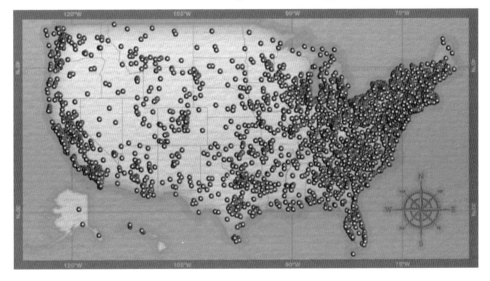

Search for your hometown history, your old stomping grounds, and even your favorite sports team.

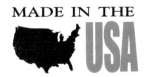